text
PAOLO PACI AND ROBERTO MOTTADELLI

editorial coordination
LAURA ACCOMAZZO

graphic design
MARIA CUCCHI

CONTENTS

INTRODUCTION

"Scientifically speaking, human beings are omnivores – creatures who eat both animal and vegetable foods. Like others of this ilk such as pigs, rats, and cockroaches, we can satisfy our nutritional needs by ingesting a broad variety of substances. We can eat and digest everything from rancid mammary gland secretions to fungi to rocks (or cheese, mushrooms, and salt if you prefer euphemisms). Like other paragons of omnivory, we do not literally eat everything..."

So begins *Good to Eat*, a successful volume written in 1985 by American anthropologist Marvin Harris. It's a biological fact that humans are omnivorous creatures, equal to great anthropomorphic simians and the less refined animal species indicated above. But, the fact that humans "do not eat literally everything" is a cultural one. The origins of food are ancient and surprising. For example, one of the most recent theories links human nutritional choices directly to their evolution, from the treetops to the earth and from quadrupeds to bipeds. Insects are responsible for this morphological revolution, together with the fruit that was fundamental to

the diets of the first hominids, whose hunting led to specialization in the higher arts of catching and manipulating small prey, as well as to the development of frontal vision. Early humans were frugivores and insectivores: a diet that helped to "invent" modern humanity but that would cause uncomfortable intestinal fermentation today, not to mention violent reactions of disgust in many people. Rich in protein and minerals, and with very little fat, insects are no longer popular on our tables (in fact this book does not contain a single recipe for larvae or locusts), even though insects on a skewer are still an expensive delicacy in much of the Eastern world.

Besides the choice of what to eat, the distinction that most separates humans from other primates is the way that food is procured. Once the motor skills required for gathering fruit and catching insects were developed, humans become more social, always through food. Nomadic hunters and gatherers combined their efforts to accumulate more calories. They organized into tribes to survive periods of scarcity. For hierarchically structured groups, the shift from nomadic living to settling in one place was short. The domestication of plants and animals began around the end of the Ice Age, about 12,000 years ago. By 2000 BC, nearly all the species still utilized today had been selected. "I have seen great surprise expressed in horticultural works at the wonderful skill of gardeners, in having produced such splendid results from such poor materials," wrote Charles Darwin in *On the Origin of Species*. But he also adds that the art of agriculture was simple: "It has consisted in always cultivating the best-known variety, sowing its seeds, and, when a slightly better variety chanced to appear, selecting it, and so onwards."

But agriculture and breeding were still a big developmental step forward compared to hunting insects. Gastronomy, the last cultural ingredient that distinguishes humans from the rest of the animal world, was born from these practices. It may have been normal to eat a juicy, raw larva dug right out of the ground, but you couldn't do the same with an ear of corn (the first species domesticated in South America) or a ram. No, with corn and rams, we adopted a different strategy,

and found a way to reduce them both to acceptable dimensions through milling or butchering, and make them digestible through various cooking methods. That is one reason why you won't find any insects in this book, but there are many recipes that call for cornmeal, lamb shank, and other similar foodstuffs.

Some researchers have said that the invention of agriculture was one of humanity's worst mistakes. Even the Bible puts forth this theory. Genesis reads, "Cursed is the ground because of you; In toil you will eat of it all the days of your life. Both thorns and thistles it shall grow for you..." Translated into modern anthropological terms, agriculture has encouraged the development of organized work, and therefore a new social hierarchy. Tom Standage summarizes in *An Edible History of Humanity*, "...agriculture is profoundly unnatural. It has done more to change the world, and has had a greater impact on the environment, than any other human activity...It overturned the hunter-gatherer way of life that had defined human existence for tens of thousands of years, prompting humans to exchange a varied leisurely existence of hunting-and-gathering for lives of drudgery and toil. Agriculture would surely not be allowed if it were invented today."

This is very true – agriculture revolutionized the natural landscape. It forced humans to eat bread made "by the sweat of [their] brow" (Genesis again). However, in exchange, we must add, it bestowed upon us an invaluable gift: gastronomy. From the beginning, this art form has defined social roles and behavior (for example in the distribution of labor within nuclear families) and encouraged economic and cultural exchange (just consider the opening of commercial routes for the spice trade). It supported the survival and development of entire civilizations. To give another macroscopic example, the historic impact of the exchange of comestible goods between East and West is incalculable. While potatoes traveled from the Americas to the Eurasian continent, sugarcane made the opposite journey and found fertile lands in the Caribbean. History informs us that the potato saved the Europeans from famine, while the intensely cultivated sugarcane provided all humanity with a valuable source of calories. Recipes involving potatoes and sugar abound in this volume.

Brillat-Savarin, the most famous writer on gastronomy of all time, is often cited: "The discovery of a new dish confers more happiness on humanity than the discovery of a new star." This quote is also appropriate in our case, and not just in terms of hedonism, because new recipes stimulate the palate and satisfy the senses. But in strictly cultural terms, gastronomy is a universal language and each new recipe is another word added to the dictionary, encouraging richer and more fertile interactions among human beings. Since the beginning of agriculture, this exchange has never ceased. Among the various African, Asian, and European techniques herein, there is a certain harmony that is not accidental. Filled dough belongs to the Chinese as much as to the Italians, and fried pastries span traditions from Southeast Asia to North Africa. Flours and semolinas, roughly round grains, couscous and bulghur are a constant in both Arab and Bantu cultures. Unleavened bread cooked on hot stones, perhaps the first recipe ever created by humans, is still made today at the foot of the Himalayas and among the dunes of the Sahara. In Oceania and the Americas, the new worlds, we witness instead the export and reinterpretation of European, Creole, and Asian recipes. This melting pot of flavors recounts, better than any storybook, the various emigrations that have occurred in the last 500 years, the slave trade, and the continuous fusion and culinary syncretism.

The language of recipes is not limited to flavors or techniques. Gastronomy is above all a community ritual, an institution of social conventions. It begins in our prehistory as an offer to the gods (in the Inca culture it was good for the new harvest). Then it transformed into pure philosophy (like the tea rite codified by Japanese master Rikyu). The study of gastronomy opens an immense field of exploration, linked to the artisanal traditions that respond to a need for cooking and table setting. It tells us of Catherine de' Medici's fork (it seems she was the one to introduce it to the French court) and the knives of the *gauchos*, used for Argentinian *asado*. It moves from the refined use of chopsticks to the simple hands that pick up food in the Horn of Africa. In the Borgia era, it became an art to sit at the table, to set it, and to receive guests there. From silver and crystal, French service (serving platters brought directly to the table) or Russian service (plates already portioned, as in a restaurant), we arrive at contemporary styles, the exhibition of culture, economic power, and status symbols. Gastronomy is all of this and more. These themes are echoed in the 120 recipes that follow, divided into five continents but united by a common history. You can read them, make them in your kitchen, order them in restaurants, or dream about them. You can eat them at home or in a tavern, at a rest stop, or in a lavish three-star dining room, aware that whether it's fast food or haute cuisine, gastronomy is always human history.

EUROPE

There's a little story behind a recipe that explains a great deal about European gastronomy: the tale of Veal Prince Orloff. Though the name refers to Prince Orloff, who was descended from a favored suitor of Catherine the Great, the recipe was really invented by the prince's chef, Urbain Dubois. It was a rich dish, full of creamy and buttery sauces (some claim this was to cover up the low quality of Russian veal). It was so complicated and time-consuming to prepare (for example, removing the veal bones and then putting them all back together, an operation no cook would dream of doing anymore) that it became one of the foremost recipes of French *grande cuisine*. It symbolizes a gastronomic tradition that emerged from the splendor of Renaissance courts, then shifted to bourgeois kitchens, and finally made its way to high-end restaurants.

This story also chronicles the rise of French chefs to stardom and celebrity. It begins with La Guypière, Napoleon's "cook", then progresses to Antonin Carême, the most famous 19th century chef (his Le *Maître d'hôtel français ou parallèle de la cuisine ancienne et moderne*, from 1822, dictated culinary rules for the entire 19th century). The trend continues today with Troisgros, Bocuse, Ducasse and all their colleagues who've earned three Michelin stars. Paradoxically, these very three rebelled against the extravagant *grande cuisine* techniques in the 1980s, signaling a return to the simplicity and freshness of seasonal flavors. Meanwhile, major continental powers continue to cross paths at the table, among the layers of Veal Prince Orloff. Caviar, for example, is yet another chapter in the history of Franco-Russian culinary relations. This "poor man's dish" from the Volga fisherman made it all the way to the table of the czar, then traveled to Paris with Russian aristocrats who emigrated after the revolution.

The supremacy of French cuisine also fostered the intellectual work of the great theorists. It began with Anthelme Brillat-Savarin, a child of Illuminism and the Restoration whose *Physiologie du goût* (1825) approached the philosophy of gastronomy for the first time, and has progressed all the way to the most feared reviewers in the modern restaurant industry, Gault and Millau, who must be included among the fathers of *nouvelle cuisine*. All of these royal and powerful people with their need for recognition— court and celebrity chefs, food critics and journalists—

THE TRUE ART OF COOKING

have turned a physiological necessity (nutrition) into a true art and lifestyle over the last two centuries.

It is in France that elite gastronomy was born, developed, renounced and restored. Just as they did for the fields of enology and *haute couture*, the French dictated the paradigm for the rest of Europe (and the world). But, we must also consider France because of Antoine-Augustin Parmentier, a culinary theorist and the man who popularized a product that literally saved Europe from famine: the potato. And so we shift from the high courts of gastronomy to the country kitchens. Parmentier was a farmer at the end of the 18th century, a time when the potato was only cultivated for decorative purposes because of its beautiful flowers, leading people to suspect that it was toxic. But Parmentier was convinced of the tuber's nutritional value, and his strategy for persuading the people of Paris to eat potatoes is famous: he planted them in the Champ de Mars. Guards watched over the plants during the day, but they were left unguarded at night. The plan worked and nocturnal "predators" wasted no time in propagating this new food. Parmentier left us so much more than a recipe for eggs and meat with boiled or mashed potatoes; his extraordinary achievement of providing the entire continent with an alternative to grains in a period of famine encouraged population growth beyond all expectations. A perfect, though negative, example of this is the notorious potato blight that wiped out all the crops in Ireland between 1845 - 1847, causing a million deaths from starvation and an increase in overseas emigration (Ireland's connection to the potato is why our collection includes a dish celebrating the tuber itself, a Gaelic colcannon recipe). Though potatoes were originally brought over from Perù and Bolivia by the Conquistadors, they were not eaten on a large scale until the end of the 18th century. They were the real "fuel" of the Industrial Revolution and the driving force behind modern European civilization.

The potato is the essential *passe-partout* of European gastronomy. It can be cultivated in extremely diverse climates, and the starchy taste goes splendidly with both fish (from *moules-frites* in all its simplicity, which is the national dish of Belgium, to Ligurian octopus with potatoes or Swedish *laxpudding*) and meat, especially traditional German pork dishes. But, there's another ingredient that's very different from the potato and opens the door to culinary traditions from a wide range of countries: cod. It's also called stockfish or *baccalà* depending on whether the preservation method involves salting or drying. The very name implies internationality, and in fact, the Spanish *bacalao* has Flemish origins (*kabeljaw*, "fish stick"). The Norwegian *stokkfisk* still refers to it as "stick fish", as opposed to the English "stock fish". The etymology of the latter is the most interesting, because the possibility of preserving it and transporting it all over is what made cod popular throughout Europe. In this collection we present a Portuguese recipe, *bacalhau à Gomes de Sà*, but this Northern fish can be cooked a thousand different ways according to various regional interpretations throughout Europe: Vizcaya-style in The Basque Country (with peppers), creamed in Veneto (with olive oil), as simple as fish and chips in Britain, or as laborious as Livornian *baccalà*.

Digging deeper into the various European culinary conventions, coincidences abound. The simplest and richest dishes are always fish-based, and the fish stews all originated as "poor men's meals" among fishermen trying to utilize any unsold, leftover fish. They're found on every coast, from Adriatic broths to *cacciucco*, to the Provençal *bouillabaisse* presented here—a recipe so often imitated that the restaurateurs of Marseilles drew up a charter to document the original formula. It uses as many types of fish as possible, with tough or soft flesh, and all types of shellfish, but nothing too expensive (lobster is a recent addition). The herbs and spices used recall the scents of the Mediterranean (fennel, orange) and the Eastern spice trade (saffron).

Those Eastern spices are also called upon in a meat dish whose many versions evoke the countries of Central Europe: Hungarian *gulyas* is also known as *pörkölt*, or *goulash* in Austria, Slovenia, and Croatia. Just as fish stews typically originate with fishermen, this "outdoor" beef stew (or soup) is a tradition among the cowboys of Puszta, who are descended from nomadic Asian populations. The dish gets its characteristic color and aroma from paprika, which is also from Asia. It was introduced to Hungarians by the Turks, who had in turn imported it from India.

Coincidences continue to crop up everywhere, often unexpectedly. Pastoral stews recur throughout Europe, utilizing whatever products might be available. In the absence of beef from the high plains, there is lamb from the more closed areas (like Serbian *djuvec*), or Finish reindeer, which is listed here. The culinary tradition we might call "country" was born in the self-sufficient farmhouses of Central Europe, providing us with high calorie pork (here you will find German glazed pig knuckle and Alsatian *choucroute*) and chicken dishes (like Slovakian duck sauce). There is also a sort of transnational current that spans the Alps and brings us melted cheeses from Savoia to Carnia, like *raclette*, fondue (the recipe here is attributed to Switzerland, home of Alpine *toma* cheeses), and *frico* (cheese crisps). We also find an abundance of butter and preserved meats, and vegetables typical of cold climates (potatoes and cabbage again). The recurrence of filled dough pockets is another curious cultural similarity. Typical of the Po valley, they are also found in the valleys of Eastern Europe. Here we provide the example of Polish *pierogi*, which can be fried or boiled.

If the European culinary panorama ended here, we would be dealing with an extremely high calorie diet that was particularly rich in protein, starch, and animal fats. Fortunately, in addition to the aristocratic mark of French *grande cuisine* and a continental country tradition, there is a third and perhaps even richer branch: Mediterranean cuisine. In contrast to the culture of butter and meat, it has become known as the healthy "Mediterranean diet." Resting upon the three pillars of olive oil, grains, and vegetables, it developed along the southern banks of the Mediterranean, including the coasts of Spain, Italy, and Greece (often called the "Garlic Belt"). This diet has been particularly strong in southern Italy, especially in Cilento, an area south of Naples where the famous American physiologist Ancel Keys lived for three decades (until he was 100 years old, becoming the greatest testimony to his own "invention"). There are numerous recipes that exemplify the Mediterranean diet, encompassing ingredients from the gardens, the fields, and the sea. Perhaps the most classic example, a food that is adored and reproduced all over the world without even changing its name, is pizza. Bread dough, tomatoes, extra-virgin olive oil, mozzarella, and basil come together in this dish to achieve a fullness of flavor and a perfect nutritional balance whose history goes back for millennia; the perfectly simple counterpoint to any fancy and complicated Veal Prince Orloff.

BACALHAU À GOMES DE SÀ

PORTUGAL

Difficulty: Medium · Time: 1 hour + reconstituting and soaking time

INGREDIENTS FOR 4 PEOPLE

1 LB (450 G) SALTED DRIED COD

1 2/3 CUPS (400 ML) MILK

12 BLACK OLIVES IN BRINE

4 POTATOES (BEST IF THEY'RE IMMATURE, OR "NEW")

2 EGGS

1 WHITE ONION

1 GARLIC CLOVE

3 TBSP EXTRA-VIRGIN OLIVE OIL

1 BUNCH OF PARSLEY

1/2 TSP GROUND BLACK PEPPER

SALT

José Luís Gomes de Sà lived sometime between the 19th and 20th centuries. Other than his passion for foods from Northern Portugal, very little is known about him. According to some, he was a merchant specializing in salted dried cod. Others say he worked as a cook at the *Restaurante Lisbonense* in Porto. What matters is that he invented this recipe, which was destined to become a hallmark of Portuguese cuisine.

Reconstitute the cod by soaking it in cold water for 2 days, changing the water every 5 - 6 hours. Then strain it and boil it for about 30 minutes. In the meantime, clean and boil the potatoes. Heat the milk and hard boil the eggs as well.

Strain the cod again and remove any bones, fins, or scales. Break it into small pieces with your hands. Put it in a bowl and pour the hot milk over it. Let it soak for at least 1 hour, then strain. As soon as the potatoes are ready (cooking time will vary based on size), strain and peel them. Slice them about 1/4 - 1/2 inch (1 cm) thick. Remove the eggshells and slice the eggs. Chop the parsley, pit the olives, and preheat the oven to 350°F (180°C).

Slice the onion into rounds and mince the garlic. Sauté them together with 2 tablespoons of oil. Turn off the heat when they start to brown. Grease a terracotta pan (or baking dish) with the remaining oil. Place a layer of potatoes in the pan and sprinkle with salt and pepper. Cover with a layer of cod. Then add a layer of sautéed onions and garlic. Continue layering in the same order (potatoes, cod, onions and garlic). Top the last layer with the olives and bake for 15 - 20 minutes. When it's done, add the parsley and egg slices and serve.

The most common variation on this recipe does not limit the vegetable sauté to onion and garlic. You can add the potatoes and cod to these ingredients and sauté everything together, mixing carefully and seasoning with salt and pepper. Then transfer it all to the terracotta pan. Don't worry about the order of the layers, just top it with olives and bake.

PAELLA VALENCIANA

SPAIN

INGREDIENTS FOR 4 PEOPLE

5 CUPS (1.2 L) VEGETABLE BROTH

2 CUPS (400 G) VALENCIA RICE
   (OR ARBORIO, OR PARBOILED)

1 LB (450 G) RABBIT

1 LB (450 G) CHICKEN

7 OZ (200 G) SPANISH WHITE BEANS, ALREADY COOKED

3/4 CUP + 1 TBSP (200 ML) TOMATO PUREE

1/3 LB (150 G) RED BELL PEPPERS

5.3 OZ (150 G) ITALIAN FLAT BEANS

8 TBSP EXTRA VIRGIN OLIVE OIL

2 PACKETS GROUND SAFFRON

1 TSP SWEET PAPRIKA

1/4 CUP + 2 TSP (70 ML) RED WINE

1/2 TSP HOT RED PEPPER
   (OR HOT PAPRIKA)

SALT

Today it's a worldwide symbol of Spanish cuisine, but *paella* was once a peasant dish with no precise recipe. It was usually cooked on Mondays to creatively use up the previous day's leftovers. This explains the numerous variations that still characterize the specialty today. The most celebrated version originated among farmers in the Valencian hinterland. Rice, vegetables, chickens, and rabbits were abundant at the time, but there were few bovine animals. Hence the standard ingredients in the Valencian recipe.

Paella would typically be made in a *paellera*, the traditional Valencian *paella* pan, but you can use a regular sauté pan or skillet as well (preferably one that's very wide and flat with low sides). Start by preparing the broth, then cut the rabbit and chicken into small pieces. Break each Italian flat bean into three pieces and slice the bell peppers. Heat the oil in a pan and add a pinch of salt. As soon as the oil is hot, add the meat and cook on medium heat for a little more than 10 minutes. Gradually pour in the wine, turning the meat to make sure it's browned on all sides. Add the Italian flat beans and the bell peppers. Cook for another 10 minutes, stirring occasionally. Add the white beans and tomato puree and mix well. As soon as all the ingredients are thoroughly combined, add the broth and the spices, including salt to taste. Carefully pour in the rice, distributing it evenly over the pan (start in the center and work quickly toward the edges). Once the rice is added, do not stir the paella anymore. Let it cook on medium-high heat for 8 minutes, then reduce the heat. Keep an eye on it and wait for all the broth to be absorbed (about 12 more minutes). Before you remove the pan from the heat, move aside a spoonful of rice to create a small "eye" in the center and check to make sure there's no more liquid left underneath. The paella should rest for a couple of minutes and be served perfectly "liquidless". If you want to serve it the traditional way, bring it to the table in the pan and fill people's plates right in front of them.

The name paella *comes from the Latin* patella, *which is also the root word for this type of pan in many modern European languages, such as the Italian* padella. Paella *originally referred to a wide, shallow, iron pan that Valencians used for dishes with rice or* fideos *(a pasta similar to spaghetti). Today the pan is called a* paellera *to avoid confusing it with the dish itself.*

CREMA CATALANA

SPAIN

Difficulty: Easy - Time: 45 minutes + cooling time

INGREDIENTS FOR 4 PEOPLE

4 EGG YOLKS
1 CUP (2.5 DL) WHOLE MILK
1 CUP (2.5 DL) HEAVY CREAM
1/2 CUP + 1 1/2 TBSP (120 G) SUGAR

2 TBSP (15 G) CORNSTARCH
1 LEMON
1 VANILLA BEAN (OR 1 TSP. VANILLA EXTRACT)
1 CINNAMON STICK

As Catalonia's most traditional dessert, this dish proudly proclaims the region's independence from foreign delicacies, particularly those from France. Though crema catalana may closely resemble them, it is not *crème caramel*, or even *crème brûlée*. Instead, it could be considered a sort of cinnamon-flavored pastry cream.

Start by grating the lemon rind. Combine the zest with the cream, milk, vanilla, and cinnamon in a saucepan. While this is heating, beat the yolks and cornstarch with 1/4 cup + 2 tablespoons + 1 teaspoon (80 g) of sugar until the mixture is smooth and creamy with no lumps.
When the contents of the pan are about to boil, remove from the heat. Strain the mixture and pour it right back into the saucepan, slowly adding the beaten yolks mixture. Cook on very low heat for 15 minutes, stirring frequently.
Pour into individual ramekins and let them cool thoroughly before putting them in the refrigerator. Refrigerate for at least 2 hours, then sprinkle the remaining sugar on top, dividing it evenly among the ramekins. Use a blowtorch to caramelize the sugar (If you don't have a blowtorch you can put the ramekins in a hot oven until the sugar forms an opaque crust).
In Catalonia, where regionalism is strong, each town takes great pride in the recipe's heritage and adds its own particular spin. One of the most common modifications is to eliminate the cream and use twice as much milk. Others use more than one egg yolk per serving, add a pinch of orange zest, or leave out the vanilla.
Before blowtorches were easy to come by, Catalan farmers heated a sort of long-handled iron over the fire and used it to caramelize the sugar. Some modern Spanish chefs still prefer this historic utensil, which surely provides more character and ambience than does its high tech counterpart.

POT-AU-FEU
FRANCE

INGREDIENTS FOR 6 PEOPLE

1.75 LBS (800 G) BEEF, CHEEK OR BOTTOM
    ROUND IS BEST

1.5 LBS (700 G) MARROW BONES

6 POTATOES

5 CARROTS

2 OR MORE GARLIC CLOVES

2 CLOVES

2 LEEKS

2 TURNIPS

2 CELERY STALKS

1 OXTAIL WITH MARROW

1 ONION

1 CABBAGE

1 BUNCH OF PARSLEY

THYME

SALT

PEPPER

When the weather starts to get cold in France, the *pot-au-feu* season begins. The recipe for this traditional dish of boiled meats and vegetables calls for beef, but there's no rule against substituting mutton or poultry, especially turkey. It takes a long time to cook and people will often use a pressure cooker to speed things up. But the great chefs recommend the traditional method, which offers more delectable results.

Rinse the beef, marrow bones, and oxtail thoroughly in cold water. Place them whole in a pot with a little more than 5 quarts (about 5 L) of lightly salted water. If you're not a big fan of marrow, wrap the bones tightly in cheesecloth so that the marrow won't seep into the liquid. Set the pot to boil and add the pepper, peeled whole onion, and cloves (many cooks choose to stick the cloves right into the onion). Boil for at least 2 hours on low heat, skimming the top every half hour to remove any impurities that float to the top.

Add the herbs and spices, turnips, and remaining vegetables, except for the cabbage, leeks, and potatoes. The potatoes should be boiled by themselves in a separate pot. After about 12 minutes, add the cabbage to the main pot. After 10 more minutes, add the leeks. Leave the main pot on low heat for another half hour, then transfer the potatoes, meat, and vegetables to one large tureen and serve.

Those who are particularly fond of marrow can skip the bone and instead add 2 tablespoons of ox marrow in the last few minutes, just before the dish is done. Ideally, pot-au-feu *should be served with toasted slices of rustic bread, mustard, and pickles. Coarse salt should always be on the table. Note that if oxtail is unavailable, substitute.*

BOUILLABAISSE
FRANCE

INGREDIENTS FOR 6 PEOPLE

3.3 LBS (1.5 KG) SCORPION FISH

2.2 LBS (1 KG) JOHN DORY

6 ANGLERFISH FILLETS

6 CONGER STEAKS

3 RED MULLETS

4 WEEVERS

2.2 LBS (1 KG) CLAMS AND/OR MUSSELS

4 RIPE TOMATOES

3 POTATOES

3 GARLIC CLOVES

3/4 CUP + 1 TBSP (2 DL) EXTRA VIRGIN OLIVE OIL

2 ONIONS

2 LEEKS

2 TBSP MINCED PARSLEY

2 BAY LEAVES

2 TSP TOMATO PASTE

2 TSP SAFFRON

1 ORANGE PEEL

1/2 TSP FENNEL SEEDS

SALT

BLACK PEPPER

Its origins are shrouded in legend, but modern *bouillabaisse* was born among the fishermen of Marseilles, who cooked it right at the port. They used nearly every species of fish they managed to catch, and as a result the recipe calls for at least four types. Scorpion fish, red mullet, and conger are the most essential. Then you can add angler, weever, John Dory, turbot, flathead mullet, dentex, European hake, etc.

Clean and scale the fish, letting any liquid drain. Fillet only those that are too large to be cooked whole. Slice the white part of the leeks and onions, crush the garlic cloves, and cut the tomatoes and potatoes into large chunks.
Pour the oil into a large pot and sauté the onions and leeks on low heat. Add the tomatoes, tomato paste, bay leaves, and orange peel. Mix well, then remove the bay leaves and orange peel. Add the shellfish (and any other small fish) and season with salt and pepper to taste. Cook for 12 minutes, stirring well. Add 2 quarts (a scant 2 L) of boiling water, parsley, and fennel seeds. After half an hour add the scorpion fish, John Dory, saffron, and potatoes. If the fish is not completely covered by the broth, add water until it's covered. Bring it back to a boil and wait 10 minutes. Then add the larger fish, first the conger then the anglerfish, and make sure they're fully immersed. After about 15 minutes, remove the smaller whole fish, the fillets, and the potatoes. Arrange them on a platter with the whole fish laid on top of the fillets. Reduce the remaining contents of the pot, then strain the broth into a soup tureen.
The secret to bouillabaisse is in the boiling - you have to turn the heat up extremely high to bring the stew back to a boil, then immediately lower it again. In fact, in Provençal (still spoken in the South of France), the name of the dish means "boil and lower".

Tradition calls for bouillabaisse *to be served with the fish on one platter and the broth in a separate bowl kept hot with a plate warmer. It's generally accompanied by toasted bread rubbed with garlic and* rouille *(a sort of mayonnaise flavored with garlic, saffron, and hot pepper).*

VEAL PRINCE ORLOFF

FRANCE

INGREDIENTS FOR 6 PEOPLE

1 (3 LBS/1.4 KG) VEAL TENDERLOIN (OR TOPSIDE)

1 1/4 CUPS (300 ML) BEEF BROTH

1 CARROT

2 ONIONS

1 CELERY STALK

2 LBS (950 G) SMOKED LARD (OR A SLAB
   OF BACON), SLICED

1/4 CUP + 1 TBSP (70 G) BUTTER

1 1/4 CUPS (300 ML) SOUBISE SAUCE

1 1/4 CUPS (300 ML) MORNAY SAUCE

1 SPRIG OF SAGE

1 SPRIG OF ROSEMARY

BASIL

THYME

Aleksej Fëdorovič Orlov (or Orloff) was a Russian diplomat and a favorite of Empress Catherine II of Russia. This dish was invented by his personal chef, a Frenchman named Urbain Dubois (1818-1901). Confronted with the slightly lower quality meat coming from Russian breeding farms at the time, he found a way to enhance it with rich sauces and condiments. The original recipe, now in the 18th Century Culinary Arts Hall of Fame, calls for an entire 22-pound (10 kg) saddle of veal. The following version has been scaled down to fit the dimensions of a modern table.

Slice the onions and dice the celery and carrot. Wrap the lard around the meat and secure it tightly with cooking twine. Melt the butter in a saucepan and sear the meat on all sides. Then add 2/3 cup (160 ml) of very hot broth along with the sage, rosemary, some thyme, and a few basil leaves. Cook on low heat for 90 minutes, slowly adding the rest of the broth throughout that time. If necessary, you can add a bit of water (which should also be very hot).
Let the meat cool, then remove the twine and cut the meat into slices about 3/4 - 1 inch (2 - 3 cm) thick. Spread Soubise sauce on each slice and reassemble the tenderloin, using more twine if necessary. Spread Mornay sauce all over the outside, along with any remaining Soubise sauce. Bake at 350°F (180°C) for 15 minutes and serve.
Veal Prince Orloff is generally accompanied by roasted new potatoes and sautéed carrots or Champignon mushrooms sautéed with butter. If you didn't use all the Mournay sauce, serve the rest with the meat.

To add more flavor, you can lard the veal before wrapping it in the smoked lard or bacon slices. To do so you'll need a larding needle to insert small strips of fat into the meat.
Soubise is a béchamel-based sauce, with a bit of butter and stewed onions added. Mornay sauce is also béchamel-based, with egg yolk, cream, and grated cheese added. You can use more of both sauces than the amount indicated in the recipe.

TARTE TATIN
FRANCE

INGREDIENTS FOR 6/8 PEOPLE
2 LBS (900 G) RENETTE OR GOLDEN DELICIOUS APPLES
1 2/3 CUPS (200 G) FLOUR
3/4 CUP (175 G) BUTTER
2/3 CUP (120 G) BROWN SUGAR, PACKED
1 LEMON
POWDERED SUGAR
SALT

According to tradition, this dessert was born in the second half of the 19th century. Sisters Stéphanie and Caroline Tatin were the owners of a hotel and restaurant in the small town of Lamotte-Beuvron. They'd forgotten the bottom layer of dough while making an ordinary apple pie, so they remedied the situation by putting the pastry dough on top of the apple mixture.

Take 6 tablespoons of butter from the refrigerator and it them sit out for at least 1 hour. When the butter has softened, cut it into small pieces. Sift the flour and a pinch of salt onto a pastry board, and create a well in the center. Place the butter pieces in the well and work them into the flour until they've been fully absorbed.
Add 1/4 cup (60 ml) of water and carefully work that in too. When the dough is consistent, wrap it in plastic and put it in the refrigerator. It has to chill for at least 1 hour before you roll it out. Juice the lemon into a bowl of water. Peel and core the apples, then slice them into 6 - 8 wedges and put them in the water. Cut the remaining butter into small pieces and heat it with the brown sugar in a round, oven-safe pan (about 9 1/2 inches/24 cm in diameter). When the sugar begins to caramelize, add the apples (make sure they've been well-strained) and cook for 10 minutes on medium heat, stirring gently. Turn off the heat and wait for the apples to cool. Meanwhile preheat the oven to 400°F (200°C) and roll the dough out to a thin disc the same size as the pan. Arrange the apple wedges so they overlap with no gaps (you shouldn't be able to see the bottom of the pan) and cover the whole thing with the dough. Bake for 15 minutes, then lower the temperature to 350°F (180°C) and bake for another 15 minutes. Take it out of the oven and flip it over onto an oven-safe plate. Sprinkle with some powdered sugar, put it back in the oven for a few minutes, and serve warm.

Putting the apples in water with lemon juice isn't essential, it's just to make sure they don't turn brown. When making the dough you can also replace the water with the same amount of milk and add an egg yolk.

COLCANNON

IRELAND

INGREDIENTS FOR 4 PEOPLE

1 LB (450 G) SAVOY CABBAGE

1 1/2 CUPS (350 ML) MILK

5 1/2 TBSP (80 G) BUTTER

4 WHITE POTATOES

1 ONION

1 SMALL CARROT

WHITE PEPPER

SALT

Colcannon is a casserole made with cabbage and potatoes, which were staples of Irish cooking for centuries. It was once eaten mainly in the fall; a ring, thimble, button, and coin were hidden inside for Halloween. According to tradition, whoever found the ring was destined for marriage. The thimble and button were symbols of spinsterhood and celibacy, and the coin meant wealth and prosperity.

Wash the potatoes well and put them in a pot of cold water. Turn on the heat, and once the water starts to boil, cook the potatoes for 30 minutes. While they cook, peel and dice the carrot and remove the core and tougher leaves from the cabbages. Rinse the remaining leaves well and cut them into thin strips. Boil them in just a little bit of water for 10 minutes.
Strain the cabbage and potatoes. Carefully dry the cabbage with a clean towel. Let the potatoes cool, then peel them and mash them with a potato masher. Preheat the oven to 350°F (180°C).
Peel and chop the onion, then sauté it in a large pan with the butter and carrot. As soon as they begin to brown, add the cabbage, the mashed potatoes, and the milk. Mix well and let it cook for 2 - 3 minutes, then transfer it all to a buttered baking dish and bake for 10 minutes. Let it sit for a minute or two and serve.

Once upon a time, the use of carrots and type of cabbage were all that varied about this recipe. "Purists" left out the carrots, and the Savoy cabbage can actually be replaced with kale. Today many versions of colcannon are enhanced with cream and bacon.

CHRISTMAS PUDDING

ENGLAND - UNITED KINGDOM

INGREDIENTS FOR 6 PEOPLE

14 OZ (400 G) RAISINS AND/OR SULTANAS (GOLDEN RAISINS)

2 3/8 CUPS (300 G) CHOPPED OR GROUND SUET, PREFERABLY FROM VEAL

1 2/3 CUPS (250 G) DRIED FRUITS AND NUTS CHOPPED FINELY (WALNUTS, HAZELNUTS, PRUNES, DATES, ETC.)

1 1/4 CUPS (250 G) SUGAR

1 1/3 CUPS (200 G) CURRANTS

2/3 CUP (100 G) CHOPPED ALMONDS

3/4 CUPS + 1 TBSP (100 G) FLOUR

1 2/3 CUPS (100 G) FRESH BREAD CRUMBS

2/3 CUPS (100 G) CANDIED CITRUS PEELS, CHOPPED

4 EGGS

2 TBSP OF GROUND SPICES (GINGER, CLOVES, NUTMEG, CINNAMON)

1 ORANGE

1 APPLE

2 TBSP BRANDY OR RUM

1 PINCH OF SALT

It's the English Christmas dessert par excellence, for which money was once no object and many spices were acquired. Families often have their own special blends of aromas and dried fruits that have been handed down over generations, so the ingredients and proportions can vary greatly.

Tradition calls for the winter's first pudding to be prepared at the start of Advent and for each member of the family to participate in the preparation.

Suet may not be easy to find and can be replaced with shortening or margarine, though this will alter the flavor slightly. To make the dessert lighter you can lower the amount of fat in the original recipe and add more bread crumbs.

Grate the entire orange rind and juice half the orange. Peel and core the apple, and chop it finely. Stir the suet, orange zest, orange juice, apple, raisins, fruit, almonds, sugar, and other ingredients together until evenly combined. Then leave it to macerate in a cool place. The best way is to wrap it in a pudding cloth and let it sit for 10 days before cooking it. But a simple mixing bowl and 3 hours of patience work well enough. If you want to make the original recipe, the important thing is to stir it at least once every 24 hours while it macerates.

When the time is up, transfer the pudding to a buttered mold and steam or cook it in a double boiler. Keep an eye on the water level and top it off when necessary. Remove it from the mold and serve it warm. The pudding can be garnished with whipped cream. On Christmas Day, it's presented with a decorative sprig of holly.

Some variations of the recipe include the juice and zest of half a lemon and about 5 oz (150 ml) of stout.

It was once very common to hide one or more silver coins in the pudding. Finding one in your plate was a sign of good luck. However, this has led to dental damage more than once, as well as children choking. So today, far fewer families keep up this ancient tradition.

COCK-A-LEEKIE
SCOTLAND - UNITED KINGDOM

INGREDIENTS FOR 4 PEOPLE
1 CHICKEN, ABOUT 3 LBS (1350 G)
1 LB (450 G) LEEKS
GENEROUS 1/2 CUP (100 G) WHITE RICE
12 PRUNES, PITTED
1 BUNCH OF PARSLEY
THYME
BLACK PEPPERCORNS
SALT

Chicken and leeks are the fundamental ingredients in cock-a-leekie, a soup that was invented to add more flavor to the meat of older chickens. It seems that prunes were originally added to make the soup more nutritious because barnyard animals were scarce. Fortunately, meatier and tenderer chickens can be used today, but the prunes have remained to enhance the flavor of the dish.

Rinse and dry the chicken, then put it in a saucepan with the parsley, a pinch of thyme, and a few peppercorns. Pour in enough water to cover everything. Season with salt, cover the pot, and cook on low heat for about 45 minutes. Every 10 minutes, use a perforated spoon to remove the fat and other impurities that float to the top.
In the meantime, slice the leeks into rounds. When 45 minutes are up, remove the chicken and strain the broth. Put the broth back on the stove on low heat to thicken a bit. Meanwhile remove the bones from the chicken and cut it into small pieces.
Put the chicken pieces into the broth along with the rice and the prunes. After 5 minutes add the leeks. Cover the pot and simmer for about 25 minutes from this point. If necessary, you can add a bit of water while it cooks. Serve nice and hot.

If you want to try a particularly flavorful cock-a-leekie, you can use broth instead of water to cook the chicken at the beginning. Other variations might use barley or other grains instead of rice. The spices used at the beginning can also vary; for example, you can add a couple of bay leaves. The dish is often served with a sprinkling of pepper and parsley.

FARIKAL
NORWAY

INGREDIENTS FOR 4 PEOPLE

1 1/3 LBS (600 G) LAMB
1 1/3 LBS (600 G) WILD CABBAGE
4 TBSP (60 G) BUTTER
1 TBSP FLOUR
1 TBSP BLACK PEPPERCORNS
PEPPER
SALT

Farikal (or more precisely *fårikål*) is a lamb and cabbage stew. Today you can find it throughout Norway at any time of year, but it was once cooked only in the southwest in the fall, when the sheep were slaughtered. Mutton had to suffice in other seasons.

Cut the meat into equal-sized pieces. Clean the cabbage and cut it into thin strips. Boil the cabbage in a pot of salted water and strain it well. Then heat the butter in a pan and sauté the meat. When it's browned on all sides, turn off the heat and transfer it to a large pot. Place alternate layers of meat and cabbage in the pot, ending with cabbage. Sprinkle each layer of cabbage with peppercorns, a bit of flour, and a pinch of salt.
Pour in enough water to cover everything. Then cover the pot and bring it to a boil. Cook on moderate heat for about 2 hours (time will vary based on the size of meat pieces). Serve hot, preferably with boiled potatoes.

In addition to a small amount of lean meat, the most traditional recipe calls for many other cuts of lamb, including those with fat and bone. If you want to try this rustic version of farikal, *which recalls a time when meat was scarce, increase the amount of meat (you'll need at least 2 lbs/900 g) to compensate for the larger amount of parts that will be discarded.*
If you prefer the more robust flavor of mutton instead, consider the possibility of longer cooking times.

LAX PUDDING
SWEDEN

Difficulty: Medium - Time: 1 hour 30 minutes + cooling time

INGREDIENTS FOR 6 PEOPLE

1.75 LBS (800 G) POTATOES

1 1/4 CUPS (300 ML) MILK

1/2 LB (250 G) SMOKED SALMON

1/4 CUP + 3 TBSP (100 ML) HEAVY CREAM

1 3/4 TBSP (25 G) BUTTER

4 TBSP + 2 TSP (15 G) DILL

4 EGGS

1 ONION

1 TBSP BREADCRUMBS

GROUND WHITE PEPPER

SALT

Lax pudding is a salmon casserole. It was often prepared for lunch as a way to use leftover salmon and boiled potatoes from the previous night's dinner. All you had to do was add a bit of milk and cream, put it in the oven, and the dish was ready. Perhaps that's why the recipe still endures and lends itself to numerous adaptations, most often concerning the main ingredient. The salmon can be steamed, boiled, smoked, or baked. You can also add different spices and even some sliced vegetables. This is a recipe for laxpudding with smoked salmon and dill.

Wash the potatoes and put them in a pot of cold salted water. Boil them for half an hour and strain. Then peel them and leave them to cool. Preheat the oven to 425°F (225°C) and cut the smoked salmon into small pieces. Slice the potatoes about 1/4 inch (0.5 cm) thick. Peel and slice the onion, chop the dill, and mix them both with the salmon and a third of the potatoes. Grease a casserole dish and line the bottom with half the remaining potatoes. Layer the salmon mixture over them. Top it with the rest of the potatoes and season with pepper.
Break the eggs into a mixing bowl. Add the milk, heavy cream, and a bit of salt. Beat them together thoroughly and pour the liquid over the top layer of potatoes. Sprinkle with breadcrumbs and dot with butter. Bake for 25 minutes.

Lax pudding *should be served with butter and* knäckebröd, *the crunchy, traditional Swedish bread made with a mix of wheat and rye flours.*

PORONKÄRISTYS

FINLAND

INGREDIENTS FOR 4/6 PEOPLE
2 LBS (900 G) REINDEER MEET (FROZEN IS FINE)
5 OZ (150 G) LARD
BLACK PEPPER (OR WHITE)
SALT

Poronkäristys is probably the most celebrated reindeer dish. A particularly tender, lean, and flavorful meat, reindeer is often eaten roasted, boiled, sautéed, dried, or smoked. But as this recipe demonstrates, it's at its best in stews.

Slice the meat into strips or small pieces. If it's frozen (it can be difficult to find fresh reindeer in many Finnish cities), cut it before it's completely thawed.

Chop up the lard (technically you should use reindeer fat) and heat it in a terracotta or cast iron pot. Once it's melted, add the meat. Mix for a few minutes with a wooden spoon and cover the pot. Make sure the bottom is never completely dry. As soon as the liquid produced by the meat dries up, add 3/4 cup (180 ml) of water and sprinkle with salt and pepper. If necessary, add more water later on, a little bit at a time.

Cook on medium heat for about 30 minutes, considering that the total time will vary depending on the size of the meat, and serve.

The most typical side dishes are mashed potatoes, pickles, spinach, beets, and especially cranberries (even in the form of jam).

You can add 1 - 2 onions to the poronkäristys *recipe: put them in the pot when you add the water, salt, and pepper. You can also substitute beer for some of the water. Certain versions also call for a bit of cream, a traditional ingredient in many Finnish recipes.*

BLINI WITH CAVIAR
RUSSIA

INGREDIENTS FOR 4 PEOPLE

1 1/2 CUPS (350 ML) HEAVY CREAM

1 1/4 CUPS (300 ML) WARM MILK

1 1/2 CUPS (170 G) BUCKWHEAT FLOUR

3.5 OZ (100 G) CAVIAR

2 TBSP (25 G) BUTTER

0.2 OZ (6 G) YEAST

2 EGGS

HALF A LEMON

1 TSP SUGAR

SALT

Compared to common savory crêpes, blini are heavier and have a more intense flavor due to the use of buckwheat flour. In Russia, they can also be served with salmon and herring, but around the world the favorite topping is caviar.

Warm up half the milk and dissolve the yeast in it. Add the sugar and 1 tablespoon of flour, and mix well until a soft batter forms. Let it rise for 2 hours at room temperature.
Meanwhile sift the remaining flour and separate the eggs.
Add the sifted flour to the batter, along with a pinch of salt, the egg yolks, and the rest of the milk. Mix until it is consistent. In a separate bowl, whip the egg whites into stiff peaks. Carefully fold them into the dough. Add 3 tablespoons (50 ml) of lightly whipped cream and let it rest for 30 minutes.
Melt the butter and used it to grease a 3-inch (8 cm) nonstick pan. Preheat the oven to a low temperature.
Heat the greased pan and pour an even layer of batter, just under 1/8 inch (3 mm) high. Cook for 2 minutes, then flip the *blini*. Cook for about 1 more minute and remove it from the pan. Put it in the oven to keep it hot, and repeat the process until all the batter is used.
Juice half a lemon, mix it with the rest of the heavy cream, and thinly slice the shallot. Serve the cream, shallot, warm *blini*, and cold caviar on separate plates.
Each diner should construct their own *blini* and eat them immediately, so the caviar doesn't absorb too much heat from the crepe.

You can replace some of the buckwheat flour with wheat flour, though exceeding 50% is not recommended. Onion can be substituted for the shallot, which is not indispensable. Even so, some versions of the recipe call for a small amount to be included in the blini *batter.*
For a lighter version, you can use yogurt instead of cream.

ROSSOLJE
ESTONIA

INGREDIENTS FOR 4 PEOPLE

1 LB (450 G) HERRING FILLETS (PICKLED
   OR MARINATED)

1 LB (450 G) SMOKED HAM (OR BACON)

1 CUP (250 ML) SOUR CREAM

4 COOKED BEETS

3 HARD BOILED EGGS

3 POTATOES, MEDIUM TO LARGE

2 RED APPLES

3 TBSP MUSTARD

1/2 TSP SUGAR

GROUND PEPPER

SALT

Rossolje (or *rossolye*) is a simple and highly nutritious salad. The core ingredients are herring fillets and beets, but it also includes eggs, apples, and sour cream—practically all the "poor man's" foods that were available in Estonia even during the winter months. Those who were able to would have added some meat as well.

Rinse the potatoes and put them in a pot of cold water. Boil them for at least 30 minutes, or until they all prove tender when a toothpick is inserted (time will vary based on size). Meanwhile hard-boil the eggs, and in a large bowl, mix the mustard, sugar, sour cream, and a pinch of salt. Stir well and set the mixture aside.
Strain the potatoes and let them cool, then peel and cube them. Remove the eggshells and cut the eggs into wedges. Dice the ham and the beets, break up the herring fillets, peel and dice the apples, and mix everything together. Sprinkle with pepper, then serve with rye bread and the sour cream and mustard dressing.

The smoked ham or bacon can be substituted with other cuts of pork, or even other types of meat (particularly lamb or beef). If you make this substitution, the meat needs to be boiled before you dice it.
You can also replace half the sour cream with heavy cream if you like. And, for a slightly different presentation, you can leave the herring fillets whole and serve the potatoes separately.

BORSCH

UKRAINE

INGREDIENTS FOR 4 PEOPLE

6 MEDIUM-SIZED BEETS

3/4 LB (400 G) TOMATOES,
   ABOUT 2 1/4 CUPS CHOPPED

1/2 LB (225 G) CABBAGE

1 1/4 CUPS WATER

2 CUPS + 5 TSP KVAS

2 CUPS + 5 TSP BEEF BROTH

1 SMALL TART APPLE

1/4 CUP DRY BEANS

4 TBSP SOUR CREAM

SALT

PEPPER

Borsch is a popular dish throughout Eastern Europe, from Romania to Poland to the Baltic States, but above all, it is a traditional specialty in Russia and the Ukraine. Beets are the main ingredient and were historically a food staple in poor, rural areas. Depending on the region and the season, various other vegetables such as carrots, potatoes, and mushrooms might be added. There are also "richer" versions of *borsch* that include beef, pork, or chicken.

Blanch and peel the beets. In another pot, boil the dry beans in the water for about 1 hour. Turn off the heat and leave them to soak until they become tender. Then add the beef broth and *kvas*.
Crush the tomatoes until they reach a puréed consistency. Slice the beets and add them to the beans along with the tomatoes. Cut the cabbage into six pieces, remove the center and add it to the pot.
Add the apple next, slicing it and removing the core and seeds. Season with salt and pepper, then cook the soup for a full 30 minutes on medium heat. A hint: to fully appreciate the taste of *borsch*, it is recommended that you dollop a bit of sour cream in the bowls first and then pour the boiling hot soup over it.

Among the ingredients is kvas, *a low-alcohol drink that's common in Russia and many other Eastern European countries. It can be produced through the fermentation of fruits, berries, or grains. Kvas that's intended for drinking (sweeter and often derived from fruits) is often distinguished from "table"* kvas, *which is used for cooking and would therefore be used in* borsch. *The latter is usually made from barley, rye, or black bread. If you can't find* kvas *(and considering the complexity of making it yourself) don't try to substitute something else. The recipe will do just fine without it.*

PIEROGI

POLAND

Difficulty: Easy - Time: 30 minutes

INGREDIENTS FOR 4 PEOPLE

1 LB (450 G) RICOTTA CHEESE

3 1/3 CUPS (400 G) FLOUR

1/3 CUP + 2 TBSP (100 G) BUTTER

2 EGGS

CHIVES

SALT

Pierogi, the traditional dumplings whose recipe might have come from Asia, were already available in the Polish royal court in the 13th century.

Very popular in Russia, Ukraine, and Belarus as well, they can be filled with mushrooms or potatoes; there's even a sweet version with fruit. The classic Polish recipe calls for a meat filling, except on Christmas Eve, when they must be made with cheese, as in the following recipe.

Mix together the flour, 1 egg, softened butter, 1 teaspoon of salt, and some warm water to help it come together. When a consistent dough has formed, transfer it to a plate and let it rest for 20 minutes.

Then roll it out to about 1/2 inch (1 cm) thick. Create circles about 2 - 2 1/2 inches (5 - 6 cm) across; you can use a glass to cut them out.

Meanwhile cut the cheese and chives. Combine them with the other egg, season with salt, and mix well.

Put a spoonful of filling into each dough circle. Fold them in half and seal the edges well.

Cook in boiling salted water until the *pierogi* float to the surface. Leave them for another 2 - 3 minutes, then take them out.

Pierogi are most commonly served with onions, smoked bacon, chives, and, especially in Russia, with sour cream. The sweet versions of the recipe (with prune, strawberry, or mixed berry filling) are best paired with whipped cream or fruit purées. Polish immigrants in North America eat sweet *pierogi* with maple syrup.

ROAST PORK WITH APPLES AND ONIONS

DENMARK

INGREDIENTS FOR 4 PEOPLE

2 LBS (900 G) PORK LOIN (WITH THE FAT STILL ON)

1 CUP (250 ML) CIDER

3 TBSP (40 ML) WHITE WINE

2 GOLDEN DELICIOUS APPLES

2 RED ONIONS

1 SPRIG OF ROSEMARY

EXTRA-VIRGIN OLIVE OIL

GROUND PEPPER

SALT

Scandanavian and German influences are united in Danish cuisine. The predilection for salmon, trout, and cod definitely comes from Northern Europe. But many pork-based dishes, like this roast with onion and apples, come from the German gastronomic tradition.

With a sharp knife, make a straight cut along the fat that covers the pork loin. Wash the rosemary and remove the needles. Mix it with salt and pepper, and rub it into the meat. Refrigerate for a few hours (or ideally overnight). Then peel the apples and cut them into thick slices. Peel and slice the onions.
Heat some oil in a large pot and brown the meat on all sides, then add the apples, onions, and cider. Cover and cook on moderate heat for about 40 minutes. Drizzle with white wine occasionally, and if necessary add a bit of water.

Another Danish dish made with apples, onions, and pork is l'æbleflæsk, which is mostly eaten in winter. Put 1 cup (250 ml) of water in a pot with 2 diced apples, 1 tablespoon of sugar, and a pinch of thyme. Simmer for 20 minutes and chop up 2/3 lb (300 g) of bacon or fatty pork. Fry the meat in another pan, then remove it and keep it warm. Brown a thinly sliced onion in the fat, mix everything together, and serve.

BAKED GLAZED PORK KNUCKLE

GERMANY

INGREDIENTS FOR 4 PEOPLE
1 1/2 CUPS (350 ML) BAVARIAN DARK BEER
1 CUP (250 ML) BEEF BROTH
4 PORK KNUCKLES
2 - 3 TBSP THYME HONEY
1 SPRIG OF ROSEMARY
GROUND PEPPER
SALT

Beer and pork are two trademarks of German cuisine. Baked pork knuckle synthesizes them in a gluttonous union, which has evolved into thousands of variations throughout the country. This is a particularly interesting interpretation due to the addition of thyme honey, which creates a mildly fragrant glaze.

Wash the rosemary, detach the needles from the stem, and mix them with some salt and pepper. Rub the mixture over the pork knuckles and refrigerate them overnight.
Preheat the oven to 325°F (160°C) and put the pork knuckles in a large pan. Pour in the broth and add enough water to make the liquid about 3/4 inch (2 cm) high.
Warm up the honey in a double boiler. Combine it with the beer, which should be room temperature, in a large bowl. Mix well, and use it to baste the pork knuckles once they've baked for 45 minutes. Repeat about every 10 minutes after that.
When they've been in the oven for 1 1/2 hours (cooking times will vary depending on the size of the pork knuckles), turn off the heat. Serve with sauerkraut and mashed potatoes (or potato salad).

The first phase of cooking can be done on the stove. Simmer the pork knuckles for almost 1 hour, in a little bit of broth diluted with water (or just plain water) and a mix of minced carrot, celery, and onion. Then transfer them to a pan with a bit of oil and some of the water they cooked in. Cook for 30 minutes, basting occasionally with beer and honey.
This recipe lends itself to various "enhancements", such as the addition of 1 tablespoon of brown sugar or a bunch of chopped parsley and a garlic clove.

CHOUCROUTE

GERMANY

INGREDIENTS FOR 8 PEOPLE

3 LBS (1.4 KG) DRAINED SAUERKRAUT

1.5 LBS (700 G) PORK LOIN

3/4 LB (400 G) SMOKED LARD (OR SMOKED BACON, OR
   SPECK HAM WITH FAT)

1/2 LB (225 G) WHITE SAUSAGE

1 CUP (250 ML) BEEF BROTH

1/3 CUP + 1 TBSP (100 ML) RIESLING WINE

3.5 OZ (100 G) GOOSE FAT (OR LARD)

10 JUNIPER BERRIES

6 STRASBOURG *KNACKS* (OR OTHER SAUSAGES)

6 MEDIUM POTATOES

4 SMOKED PORK CHOPS

2 ONIONS

2 CARROTS

1 SOUR APPLE

1 GARLIC CLOVE

1 BAY LEAF

CLOVES

SALT

PEPPER

Choucroute is a specialty from Alsace, a border region where French and German influences meet. The name comes from the Frenchification of the local expression *sürkrüt*, which in turn derives from the German *sauerkraut* ("sour cabbage"). Popular on both sides of the Rhine, this delightful dish challenges the palate with the sour taste of cabbage, then tempers it with the flavors of various sausages (like *knacks* and white sausages) and various cuts of pork.

Since the juniper berries, bay leaves, garlic, and cloves are not to be eaten, they are often tied up in a small, clean cloth for cooking, then removed at the end.
Chop the carrot and onion, and stew them with the goose fat in a large saucepan on low heat. After a few minutes, add the *sauerkraut*. In the meantime, heat the broth, and peel and cube the apple. After 10 minutes, add the wine, apple, bay leaves, garlic, a few cloves, and the juniper berries to the sauerkraut mixture. Then add the broth. Season with salt, cover the pot, and cook for 1 hour on low heat. In another pan, brown the white sausages and *knacks* for 3 minutes. Then stir the *sauerkraut* and add the white sausages, *knacks*, smoked lard (cut into chunks), pork chops, and pork loin. Cook for another 1 1/2 hours, adding a bit of water if the broth is being absorbed too quickly. While it cooks, peel the potatoes. Add them to the stew and cook for another 30 minutes, then transfer it to a serving plate and bring it to the table.

The white sausages and knacks *can be cooked separately, then added to the* choucroute *just before serving. Other cuts of pork can also be cooked separately, particularly the shoulder and foot, which are sometimes served with this dish.*

SMOKED HERRING SALAD

NETHERLANDS

INGREDIENTS FOR 4 PEOPLE

2/3 LB (300 G) GREEN BEANS

4 SMOKED HERRING FILLETS

3 YELLOW POTATOES

2 EGGS

1 - 2 SHALLOTS

1 BUNCH OF PARSLEY

2 TBSP EXTRA-VIRGIN OLIVE OIL

1 TBSP APPLE CIDER VINEGAR

PEPPER

SALT

The European culinary tradition includes numerous herring-based dishes. The salads alone are infinite, from Scandinavia to Sicily. The many versions of this dish can sometimes differ dramatically throughout The Netherlands, where herring is practically the national dish. The following is one of the simplest and best-tasting recipes, which can also include other vegetables.

Wash and clean the green beans, removing the ends and strings, and cut up the larger ones. Rinse the potatoes well under cold running water.

Steam the green beans and potatoes separately. The beans will take about 15 - 20 minutes, while the potatoes will need 30 - 40 (time will vary based on size). Check if they're done by inserting a toothpick, which should easily pierce through. Let them cool once they're cooked, then peel and dice them.

(If you don't have a steamer you can use a pressure cooker with a basket and just a little bit of water. Cook the green beans for about 3 minutes and the potatoes for about 15 - 20, counting from when the pot starts to whistle.)

Meanwhile peel and slice the shallot, mince the parsley, hard-boil the eggs, and cut the herring fillets into slices about 3/4 inch (2 cm) thick. If you prefer, you can remove the herring skin and break up the fish with your hands.

Cut the hard-boiled eggs into wedges, then put everything into a large salad bowl and sprinkle with parsley. Dress the salad with oil, salt, pepper, and apple cider vinegar.

Herring has always played a primary role in the gastronomy (and economy) of The Netherlands. Large-scale trading began in the 14th century, when a new salting and drying process was invented. They are a cornerstone of Dutch cuisine to this day, and there's even a saying that goes: haring in't land, dokter aan de kant, *or "a herring a day keeps the doctor away".*

MOULES-FRITES
BELGIUM

INGREDIENTS FOR 4 PEOPLE
4 LBS (1.8 KG) MUSSELS
4 1/4 CUPS (1000 ML) VEGETABLE OIL
2 LBS (900 G) POTATOES (YELLOW FLESH IS BEST)
2/3 CUP (160 ML) DRY WHITE WINE
2 GARLIC CLOVES
1 BUNCH OF PARSLEY
SALT

In Belgium, *moules-frites* are served in the most elegant restaurants as well as at everyday fried food stands, a concrete example of how this simple and low cost dish consisting of mussels and potatoes has conquered all palates and become a symbol of the country's "democratic" gastronomy. It's even reached beyond the borders, as *moules-frites* are also a favorite in much of northern France.

If they aren't already cleaned, wash the mussels under running water, removing all the beards and throwing away those that are already opened.
Peel the potatoes and cut them into 1/4 - 1/2 inch (1 cm) sticks. Rinse them under running water and carefully pat them dry.
Put the garlic, parsley, and mussels in a large pot. Turn on the heat and wait 2 - 3 minutes, then pour in the white wine and cover the pot. Cook until the mussels open, then remove the garlic and keep the mussels hot.
In the meantime, pour the oil into a large pot. When it reaches 300°F (150°C), add the potatoes a few at a time. Cook for 10 minutes, then remove them with a perforated spoon and turn up the heat. When the oil reaches 350°F (180°C), put the potatoes in for another 2 minutes (or until they appear crispy and golden). Then remove them and drain off any excess oil by placing them on a plate lined with paper towels. Season with salt and serve them hot with the mussels.

Peeling the garlic is not recommended for this recipe. It's better for the cloves to stay "clothed" so that their aroma is released in a more delicate manner. If you prefer thinner fries (or just want to accelerate the cooking process), cut the potatoes into sticks about 1/8 - 1/4 inch (0.5 cm) thick and fry them directly in 350°F (180°C) oil.

GOOSE BREAST AND HOUSKOVÉ KNEDLÍKY

SLOVAKIA

INGREDIENTS FOR 4 PEOPLE

Houskové knedlíky
4 CUPS + 2 1/2 TBSP (500 G) WHOLE WHEAT FLOUR
1 CUP (250 ML) MILK
8 SLICES OF STALE BREAD (BAGUETTE IS BEST)
2 EGG YOLKS
3 1/2 TSP (16 G) YEAST
1 BUNCH OF PARSLEY
SALT

Goose Breast
1 (1.3 LB/600 G) GOOSE BREAST, CLEANED AND HALVED
1/4 CUP (60 ML) FORTIFIED WINE
4 TBSP (40 G) GOOSE FAT (OR BUTTER)
2 TOMATOES
1 LEEK
1 CARROTS
1 SHALLOT
EXTRA-VIRGIN OLIVE OIL
SALT - PEPPER

Popular in Slovakia, the Czech Republic, and Germany, this was once a traditional fall dish prepared for the Feast of St. Martin. This recipe unites two fundamental ingredients from these countries' culinary traditions: goose and *knedlíky*, large sliced dumplings that can be prepared in a variety of ways.

Chop the parsley and cube the bread (if it's not hard and stale enough, bake it briefly in the oven). Sift the flour into a large mixing bowl and add the yeast and parsley. In another bowl, combine the milk, egg yolks, and a pinch of salt. Pour the egg and milk mixture into the flour and yeast, and mix well (the resulting dough should not be sticky). Cover with a towel and let it rise for at least 1 hour.
Meanwhile preheat the oven to 350°F (180°C). Rinse the goose breast, pat it dry, and brown it in a pan with a little bit of the fat (or butter). Season with salt and pepper. When it's thoroughly browned, transfer the meat to a baking dish and bake for 10 - 15 minutes. Then put it back in the pan with the rest of the fat. Add the wine and cook on low heat until the sauce thickens. Dice the tomatoes, slice the other vegetables into rounds, and sauté them all together with a bit of oil.
Take the dough you made earlier and stir it again, adding the bread cubes a few at a time. Transfer it to a work surface and shape it into cylinders about 2 - 3 inches (6 - 8 cm) in diameter and twice as long. Boil them for 25 minutes, stirring and covering the pot halfway through. Then remove them with a perforated spoon and slice them. Combine the meat, vegetables, and sliced *houskové knedlíky*, and serve them all hot.

It can be difficult to coordinate the cooking times for the meat, vegetables, and houskové knedlíky. *The best advice is to prepare the latter a bit early and keep them warm. For a bit more flavor, you can add a pinch of nutmeg to the dough, along with a sliced, sautéed onion. You can also fry the bread cubes in a bit of melted butter before adding them. The dish is generally served with baked apples and red cabbage.*

VEAL PÖRKÖLT

HUNGARY

INGREDIENTS FOR 4 PEOPLE

1.3 LBS (600 G) VEAL, SHOULDER IS BEST

3.5 OZ (100 G) LARD

3 TBSP + 1 1/2 TSP (30 G) SWEET PAPRIKA

2 ONIONS

1 GREEN BELL PEPPER

1 TOMATO

SALT

PEPPER

Pörkölt, a traditional Hungarian stew, is known to the rest of the world as *goulash*. The Magyar word *gulyás* actually refers to a different dish, a sort of meat and vegetable stew. The similarity between the two recipes, coupled with the fact that paprika is a fundamental ingredient in both, has created some linguistic confusion among foreigners that remains to this day.

What follows is the recipe for a lighter version of *pörkölt* – the veal doesn't require any particular seasoning. But there are other interpretations of the dish, ideal for more savory meats like roe deer or lamb, that use a lot of spices and involve slightly longer cooking times.

Dice the meat into 1-inch (3 cm) pieces. Peel and thinly slice the onions. Heat the lard in a large pot and cook the onion on low heat. As soon as it starts to brown, turn off the heat. Let it cool for a minute, then add the paprika and stir. Add the meat, season with salt, and turn the heat back on low. Brown the meat on all sides, then add just under 1/2 cup (100 ml) of water and cover the pot. Cook for about 15 minutes. Meanwhile, peel and slice the tomato. Dice the bell pepper or slice it into thin strips, removing the seeds. When the 15 minutes has passed, add the bell pepper and tomato to the pot. Season with ground pepper, cover again, and cook for another 20 minutes. Add 2 tablespoons of water (a little bit at a time) if the *pörkölt* starts to dry out. If the liquid seems too thin at the end, uncover the pot and cook it for a few more minutes.

The dish is generally served with boiled potatoes or noodles.

Pörkölt *can be seasoned with many different spices, especially cumin, thyme, and marjoram. You can also add 1 - 2 minced garlic cloves at the same time as the tomato and bell pepper, and use beef broth instead of water. Some versions don't call for tomato at all, adding another bell pepper instead.*

KÄSESPÄTZLE

AUSTRIA

INGREDIENTS FOR 4 PEOPLE

2 CUPS (250 G) FLOUR

1/2 LB (225 G) EMMENTALER CHEESE

3/4 CUPS (180 ML) MILK

1/2 CUP + 2 TBSP (150 G) BUTTER

2 EGGS

1 - 2 ONIONS

1 TBSP EXTRA-VIRGIN OLIVE OI

1 TSP SALT

NUTMEG

Spätzle are soft noodles made with egg and flour that are very common in Austria, Switzerland, southern Germany, and even High Adige. They can be eaten as a side dish (with baked meat and wild game) or entrée. *Käsespätzle*, which is *spätzle* with a generous topping of cheese and onion, is the latter.

Peel the onion and slice it very thinly. Grate the cheese, and set it aside with the onion. Combine the flour, egg, oil, salt, a pinch of nutmeg, and 2/3 cup (150 ml) of milk in a bowl. Mix with a whisk until the consistency is smooth. Keep in mind that the dough should fall off in large chunks when scooped up with a wooden spoon. Add the rest of the milk very gradually (if the flour is too wet there might be some left over; if it's too dry you might need to add some water). Let it rest for 10 minutes.

Boil a pot of salted water, and in a separate pan brown the onion with the butter. When the water is hot, pass the dough through a pasta machine for shaping *spätzle*, letting the noodles fall directly into the water. If you don't have one, any perforated surface with holes about 1/8 - 1/4 inch (0.5 cm) wide will work. Push the dough through the holes and cut it just after it comes out the other side. Another alternative is to spread the dough on a wet wooden cutting board (best if it has sharp corners). With a wet spoon, scrape off small strips of equal size and throw them in the boiling water. Cook until they float to the surface (3 minutes should suffice). Remove them with a slotted spoon and transfer them to a bowl. Arrange them in layers, spreading cheese between them. Top with the onion and butter and serve warm.

For a lighter version, you can use water in the dough instead of milk. Spätzle *also lend itself well to other toppings. In addition to grated cheese, melted butter, chives, cream, and speck ham are very common.*

FONDUE SUISSE

SWITZERLAND

INGREDIENTS FOR 4 PEOPLE

2 LBS (900 G) SLICED WHITE BREAD, PREFERABLY DAY-OLD

1 LB (450 G) GRUYÈRE CHEESE

1 LB (450 G) VACHERIN FRIBOURGEOIS CHEESE

1 1/2 CUPS (350 ML) FENDANT WINE (OR PINOT GRIGIO)

1/4 CUP (60 ML) KIRSCH

2 GARLIC CLOVES

4 TSP CORNSTARCH

GROUND PEPPER

Cheeses are among the most excellent products of Swiss gastronomy. *Fondue suisse* (also called *moitié-moitié*) is perhaps the best celebration of Gruyère and Vacherin Fribourgeois cheeses. Other noble cheeses such as Sbrinz, Appenzeller, and Emmentaler are the basis for similarly tasty recipes, which are simple to prepare if you have happen to have a table top burner and a *caquelon* (a small cast iron, terracotta, or porcelain saucepan), in addition to suitably long forks.

Cube the bread, peel the garlic, and remove the cheese rinds. Grate the Gruyère and dice the Vacherin Fribourgeois. Vigorously rub the inside of the *caquelon* with garlic, then mince both cloves. Separately mix the *Kirsch* with the cornstarch.
Combine the garlic, grated cheese, and wine in the *caquelon*. Bring it to a boil on medium heat, stirring continuously. Then add the *Kirsch* and cornstarch mixture. After a few seconds, reduce the heat and add the Vacherin with a sprinkling of pepper. Let the cheese melt, stirring well.
Turn on the table top burner, keeping the heat on medium-high. Transfer the *caquelon* to the burner and bring it to the table immediately, along with the cubed bread. The diners can dip the bread in the fondue pot, using the long forks. Serve with wine (Fendant or Pinot Grigio) or black tea.

Kirsch *is a cherry brandy used to flavor chocolate as well as fondue in Switzerland. And, chocolate is the main ingredient in another type of fondue,* fondue au chocolat, *which involves dipping pieces of fruit (especially apples, pears, pineapples, and bananas). If you like, you can serve some chopped fruit along with the bread for* fondue suisse.

RISOTTO ALLA MILANESE

ITALY

INGREDIENTS FOR 4 PEOPLE

4 1/4 CUPS (1 L) BEEF BROTH

2 CUPS (360 G) RICE

1/2 CUP (120 ML) WHITE WINE (PREFERABLY DRY)

1/2 CUP (50 G) PARMIGIANO REGGIANO CHEESE, GRATED

1/3 CUP (80 G) BUTTER

1.4 OZ (40 G) OX MARROW

1/4 TSP (0.2 G) SAFFRON

HALF AN ONION

In Italy, there are many recipes for rice with saffron, but practically the entire peninsula associates these ingredients with *risotto alla milanese*. The most distinctive ingredient is ox marrow, and without it this traditional Milanese dish loses it's authenticity. Forerunners of this recipe already existed in the 16th century, even though the recipe used today was formulated in the late 18th century (it was officially documented by Giovanni Luraschi in 1829, in the book *Nuovo cuoco milanese economico*).

Boil the marrow bone in a little bit of water so that the skin will come off easily (2 - 3 minutes of boiling should suffice). Chop up the marrow and melt it together with half the butter. Thinly slice the onion and add it to the marrow. When the onion has softened, add the rice and let the onion brown (the rice should be almost transparent). Pour in the wine and wait for it to absorb completely. Then add the hot beef broth one ladleful at a time, letting the rice absorb it. Cook for about 10 minutes.
Meanwhile, dissolve the saffron in some of the broth. Add it to the rice and cook it all together (about another 10 - 12 minutes), stirring to keep the rice from sticking to the pan. When the rice is *al dente*, remove it from the heat. Add the grated cheese and the rest of the butter. Cover the pan and let it sit for a few minutes before serving.

The best rice for risotto with saffron is superfine Arborio or Carnaroli. As for the broth, beef is preferable to other types.
The wine is the most "discussed" ingredient, which may have been added to the original recipe at a later date. In Monza and Brianza, not far from Milan, red wine is used instead of white. They also add Luganega sausage, often to the further detriment of the saffron.

BUCATINI ALL'AMATRICIANA

ITALY

Difficulty: Easy - Time: 35 minutes

INGREDIENTS FOR 4 PEOPLE

3/4 LB (340 G) BUCATINI PASTA
2/3 LB (300 G) RIPE TOMATOES (PLUM TOMATOES ARE
   BEST)
1/3 LB (150 G) GUANCIALE (CURED PIG'S CHEEK)
2/3 CUP (60 G) PECORINO CHEESE, GRATED
1 DRIED HOT RED PEPPER
HALF AN ONION
EXTRA-VIRGIN OLIVE OIL
SALT

The sauce described in the following recipe is named for the small town of Amatrice, which is now part of the Lazio region. Romans are truly passionate about their *amatriciana*, a dish that has always been considered a symbol of the capital's region.
It seems the recipe actually originated in the Abruzzi Appenines, where it was prepared without the tomatoes (the town of Amatrice was part of the Abruzzo province of Aquila until the 1920s). Today it's popular throughout Italy, but bucatini is not the only pasta used. It's not unusual to find spaghetti or linguini *all'amatriciana*, though these are still long form pastas.

Scald the plum tomatoes in boiling water. Remove the skin and seeds, and dice them. Dice the *guanciale* as well and fry it in 2 tablespoons of extra-virgin olive oil until it's thoroughly browned (the fat should be almost transparent).
Finely slice the onion and sauté it in the same oil as the *guanciale* (which should first be removed and drained). Before the onion starts to brown, add the diced tomatoes and the hot pepper. Cook on high heat for about 10 minutes and boil the bucatini in a pot of salted water. Cooking time will vary depending on the brand of pasta (it should be indicated on the box), but it's usually about 8 - 10 minutes. As soon as the pasta is cooked, strain it and add the tomato sauce and *guanciale*. Sprinkle with grated Pecorino and serve while hot.

If you can't find guanciale *you can substitute* pancetta, *as a large number of non-purist restaurateurs now do. Essentially,* guanciale *is just* pancetta *that's made from pork cheek.*
A "summer" version of the dish calls for cherry tomatoes instead of plum tomatoes, and the addition of spices like oregano and thyme.

PIZZA MARGHERITA

ITALY

INGREDIENTS FOR 4 PEOPLE

4 CUPS (500 G) ALL-PURPOSE FLOUR
2 CUPS (300 G) PEELED TOMATOES
2 TBSP (15 G) SUGAR
2 TBSP (15 G) BREWER'S YEAST
3.5 OZ (100 G) FRESH COW'S MILK MOZZARELLA
EXTRA-VIRGIN OLIVE OIL
BASIL
SALT

The story of this recipe has become legendary, though it does have a precise birthdate: 1889. That year, a Neapolitan pizza maker named Raffaele Esposito made three types of pizza for Queen Margherita of Savoy to sample during her visit to Naples. The queen so loved the simplicity of the tomato and mozzarella version that the specialty bore her name from that day on. And this being so soon after the Unification of Italy, it seems the pizza's fate was also decided by the chromatic combination of white (mozzarella), red (tomato), and green (basil)—the colors of the Italian flag.

Dissolve the yeast in a bowl with a little bit of warm water. Measure the flour onto a work surface and create a well. Pour the dissolved yeast, salt, and sugar into the center. Start mixing it all together, slowly adding about 2/3 cup (160 ml) of warm water, until the dough is smooth and elastic. If it's too sticky, add a bit more flour. Shape the dough into a ball and place it on a floured plate. Score the top with 2 perpendicular cuts to form a cross. Let it rise, covered, for about 1 hour (the dough should expand considerably during this time). Roll the dough out by hand or with a rolling pin, until it's about 1/8 - 1/4 inch (5 mm) thick.
Drain and chop the tomatoes, then spread them on the pizza. Thoroughly drain the mozzarella (ideally it should sit in the strainer for 15 minutes beforehand), dice it, and spread it on the pizza. Sprinkle with extra virgin oil and top it off with a few basil leaves.
Bake for about 5 minutes in a very hot wood-fired oven. If you don't have one, prepare the pizza right on a baking sheet and bake it in a very hot traditional oven (at least 230°C/450°F) for 10 - 15 minutes.

The wood-fired oven, the quality of fresh cow's milk mozzarella, and the freshness of the ingredients are among the many secrets of good Neapolitan pizza. It's possible to recreate the same crispiness with a little modification - let the pizza rise for about 1 hour after the toppings have been added. Another simple change to achieve a more particular flavor would be to use buffalo mozzarella instead of the cow's milk variety. But, if you do so, you'll need to be even more careful about draining it thoroughly.

CASSATA SICILIANA
ITALY

Difficulty: Medium - Time: 1 hour + refrigeration time

INGREDIENTS FOR 8 PEOPLE

1LB (450 G) SHEEP'S RICOTTA

1 LB (450 G) SPONGE CAKE (4 ROUND LAYERS)

2 1/2 CUPS (300 G) POWDERED SUGAR

7 OZ (200 G) CANDIED FRUIT, CUBED

3.5 OZ (100 G) BITTERSWEET CHOCOLATE

1.75 OZ (50 G) CRUSHED PISTACHIOS, A LITTLE UNDER
   1/2 CUP

1 TBSP (15 ML) RUM

3/4 TSP (2 G) GROUND CINNAMON

0.035 OZ (1 G) VANILLA POWDER,
   OR 2 TSP VANILLA EXTRACT

WHOLE CANDIED FRUIT

ORANGE FLOWER WATER

Cassata is the epitome of traditional Sicilian desserts, and along with *cannoli* it's the region's most famous confection. Both recipes are based on one central ingredient: ricotta, which must be from sheep's milk to make authentic Sicilian *cassata*, a dessert that was originally made for the Easter holidays only. The dish owes a great deal to the Arabic culinary tradition, not just for the skillful and harmonious blend of ingredients, but also for the name—*cassata* actually comes from the Arabic *quas'at*, meaning "large bowl".

Sieve the sheep's ricotta, which must be very fresh, and mix almost all of it with powdered sugar, cinnamon, vanilla and rum. Blend with a wooden spoon until it becomes a soft and smooth cream. Break the chocolate into bits and add to the mixture, together with cubes of candied fruit and crushed pistachios.

Slice the sponge cake horizontally into 4 layers of equal height. Line a deep, round cake pan (ideal size is 9 1/2 inches/24 cm) with parchment paper and place the first layer of sponge cake on the bottom. Use the second layer to line the sides of the pan. Pour half the ricotta mixture into this sponge cake base, then cover it with the third layer. Pour the rest of the ricotta on top of the third layer and cover that with the fourth layer of sponge cake.

Refrigerate the *cassata* for at least 3 hours, then take it out and invert it onto a plate.

Mix the orange flower water with the remaining powdered sugar and pour the mixture over the entire dessert, covering the sides as well. Once the glaze hardens you can decorate the *cassata* with candied fruit, whole or in strips, and create any design you like.

Some versions call for a green pistachio glaze rather than the white one described above, or Maraschino (a sweet Sicilian liqueur) instead of rum.

To avoid making an already complex specialty more difficult, this recipe calls for ready-made sponge cake. If you prefer to make your own, it's best to bake the sponge cake the day before you make the cassata.

DJUVEC

SERBIA

INGREDIENTS FOR 4 PEOPLE

1.65 LBS (750 G) LAMB LOIN CHOPS	HALF A YELLOW BELL PEPPER
3 CUPS (750 ML) LIGHT BEEF BROTH	1 EGGPLANT
3/4 CUP + 1 TBSP (150 G) LONG-GRAIN RICE	1 GARLIC CLOVE
4 POTATOES	3 TBSP LARD (OR OIL)
2 ONIONS	GROUND BLACK PEPPER
2 GREEN BELL PEPPERS	THYME
HALF A RED BELL PEPPER	SALT

Highly popular in the Balkans, *djuvec* is a dish with many variations that has found its true home in Serbia. It's a one-plate meal consisting of rice, meat, and vegetables. Every cook, professional or amateur, interprets the recipe as he or she sees fit, based on region, season, and family tradition. What follows is one of the recipes for *djuvec* with lamb.

Mince the garlic, slice the onions into rings, and dice the eggplant. Clean the peppers, removing the seeds, and slice them into thin strips. Then peel the potatoes and slice them into rounds 1/8 - 1/4 inch (0.5 cm) thick.
Rinse the rice and set it aside. Rinse the meat, pat it dry, and cut it into relatively small pieces. Heat the broth in the meantime.
Melt the lard in a large heavy-bottomed saucepan and sauté the garlic and onion. As soon as they start to brown, add the meat and cook it on all sides, keeping the heat on medium and stirring frequently. When the meat is thoroughly browned, add the rice, vegetables, and hot broth. Season with salt, pepper, and a pinch of thyme, then cover the saucepan.
Cook for about 40 minutes on low heat, and add a bit of water if the broth is being absorbed too quickly. The *djuvec* should be brought to the table hot and served directly from the saucepan.

People will often use hot water instead of broth for this recipe. In another version, the cooking process begins on the stove, then continues in the oven at 350°F (180°C). The saucepan is transferred to the oven as soon as the contents begin to boil, after the vegetables and broth have been added.
Many other vegetables can be added to djuvec, *but carrots, pumpkin, and especially tomatoes deserve a mention here. If you're cooking on the stove, the tomatoes should be peeled, diced, and added to the* djuvec *about 25 - 30 minutes after the broth. If you're using the oven, the tomatoes should be added together with the other vegetables. Lastly, you can add a teaspoon of hot paprika (or a minced hot pepper) along with the ground black pepper.*

MOUSSAKA
GREECE

INGREDIENTS FOR 6 PEOPLE

2 LBS (900 G) EGGPLANT

1 1/3 LBS (600 G) TOMATOES

1 LB (450 G) BEEF OR LAMB, CHOPPED

1 CUP (250 ML) BÉCHAMEL SAUCE

7 OZ (200 G) FETA CHEESE

2/3 CUP (160 ML) EXTRA-VIRGIN OLIVE OIL

2 ONIONS

COARSE SALT

FINE SALT

PEPPER

Moussaka could be defined as the Greek version of the more well-known Sicilian recipe for eggplant parmesan. This purple vegetable is in fact the main ingredient, and because of *moussaka* it's very popular throughout the Eastern Mediterranean, the Balkans, and the Middle East.

But it was Greece that gave it worldwide fame: the current version of the recipe is attributed to Greek chef Nikolaos Tselementes, who introduced béchamel sauce to his home country after working in Paris.

Wash the eggplants and slice them lengthwise. Sprinkle the slices with coarse salt and let them drain for about 1 hour. Chop the onions and peel the tomatoes.

Heat 1 tablespoon of extra-virgin olive oil in a pan and add the onion. When it's browned, add the chopped meat. Then add the tomatoes, fine salt, pepper, and a pinch of cinnamon. Cook on low heat for 15 minutes.

Dry the eggplant slices. In another pan with the remaining oil, brown them on both sides. Meanwhile cut up the feta cheese. Alternate layers of eggplant and meat in a large baking dish, covering each layer with a bit of feta and béchamel. Then pour the remaining béchamel sauce over the whole thing. Bake for about 1 hour in an oven preheated to 350°F (180°C), until the moussaka is thoroughly cooked. Let it sit for a few minutes before serving.

Among the different areas of the Mediterranean where moussaka *is made, and within Greece itself, there are varying interpretations regarding some of the secondary ingredients. People might add other vegetables (usually zucchini and potatoes), or spices (like cilantro, hot pepper, anise, or mustard seeds). The cheese can vary as well. Pecorino is a great substitute for feta, while the amount of béchamel sauce (or making it at home instead of buying it) is left to personal taste.*

TZATZIKI

GREECE

Difficulty: Easy - Time: 30 minutes + draining time

INGREDIENTS FOR 4 PEOPLE

2 CUPS + 1/2 TBSP (500 G) GREEK YOGURT
5 TBSP EXTRA-VIRGIN OLIVE OIL
3 GARLIC CLOVES
1 CUCUMBER
DILL
SALT

This sauce has ancient origins and is omnipresent not only in Greece, but also in Turkey (the word *cacik* is of Turkish origin) and in Armenia. It's known by other names in Serbia, Bulgaria, Cypress and Iran as well. *Tzatziki* is simple and versatile, and lends itself to many variations. But the original recipe that's closest to the cold sauce of the Ancient Greeks calls for only a few traditional ingredients.

Roughly grate the cucumber into a colander, including the skin. Let it drain for an hour (some people like to add salt to facilitate the elimination of water). Crush the garlic cloves in a mortar until they reach a creamy consistency. Pour the Greek yogurt (denser and less tart than other kinds; in Greece it's usually made from sheep's milk or goat's milk) into a bowl and mix in the garlic, oil, and cucumber. Finish it off with a sprig of dill and add salt to taste.
To really maximize the flavor, *tzatziki* should sit for an hour before serving. It will also keep in the refrigerator for several days.
This sauce is often served with black olives, and those who prefer a tangier version can add a spoonful of vinegar. Other interpretations include the addition of mint, onion, or paprika (though you risk losing the original flavor). In the Balkan States, where it is known as *tarator*, the cucumbers are fully dried out and crushed walnuts are added.

Tzatziki is normally served as a sauce with other traditional Greek dishes, such as souvlaki (skewers of meat) and gyros (marinated, spit-roasted pork). But it can also be eaten on its own, especially as an appetizer with pita or other types of bread.

AFRICA

A Qur'anic verse (5:5) reads: "This day [all] good foods have been made lawful, and the food of those who were given the Scripture is lawful for you and your food is lawful for them." The Maghreb of North Africa (Tunisia, Algeria, and Morocco) is largely Muslim, as is Egypt and the rest of the Sahara. And, the region's gastronomic offerings are always pleasing and stimulating to the Western palate. It's intriguing that in the verse quoted above, the phrase "good food" is a translation from the term *âlTayybbât*, which literally means "clean and pure things". Cooking and eating good food is a spiritual act for many Muslims, and in fact, the same verse continues, "...And whoever denies the faith—his work has become worthless, and he, in the Hereafter, will be among the losers." When entering a restaurant or supermarket in North Africa, we know that a system of Qur'anic rules and regulations takes precedence over the food itself, which is classified as *halâl* (lawful, permitted), *harâm* (unlawful, prohibited), *mashbuh* (doubtful, abstinence is preferable), and *makrûh* (detested). The Qur'an contains 40 references to good and bad food products, 12 references to table etiquette (and even more to ritual butchering), seven to hunting, and five to drinking. In short, it's a complicated subject. Though perhaps in comparison to "those who were given the Scripture" (Hebrews, who abide by kosher restrictions), things are simpler for Muslims: only pork and alcohol are truly *makrûh*, and forbidden. Interpretations have naturally proliferated over time, and today devout Muslims can refer to organizations like the Islamic Food and Nutrition Council of America for what is acceptable and unacceptable in terms of food products. The institution is highly informed, perhaps more than any imam, about diglycerides (doubtful) and monosaccharides (lawful).

We can assume that everything eaten in North Africa is *halâl*, and concentrate on the region's gastronomic history, which is perhaps even more remote than that of Europe. The oldest known collection of recipes written in Arabic dates back to the 11th century. As a result of territorial conquests and the vast trading network

A MELTING POT OF CULINARY CULTURES

established by the Arabs after Muhammad's death (under the Umayyad caliphate, the entire Maghreb, all the Middle East, and the Iberian peninsula had become Muslim by 750 AD), the Islamic world incorporated alimentary products and practices from many diverse populations. For example, honey was adopted from the Romans and was even lauded in the Qur'an, while sugarcane came from India and led to the growth of an entire industry. Today sugar and honey are still used in many North African meat and legume dishes, as well as traditional desserts. Most spices also came from India, as did rice, and both are very important in modern Arabic cooking. Preservation methods like smoking and curing came from the Byzantines. Arab "conquerors" were hungry for "good food" and did not hesitate to import new foodstuffs from conquered countries, even sausages (not pork) from Lucania, which were renamed *laqâniq* (known as *luganeghe* throughout Italy).

We've compiled some classic North African recipes in this collection. The first specialty we present is a Berber dish par excellence: *couscous*, steamed and coarsely ground semolina that's served with meat and vegetables. It's so popular that in Arabic it's also known simply as ta'am, or "food". Tasty and easy to prepare, couscous was a great success and spread to many countries. Traditionally served with fish in Sicily, it had already been "sighted" in Provence in the 17th century and was even incorporated into a Livornian lamb dish. *Couscous* is normally served with a hot red sauce called harissa, which is made with peppers, garlic, olive oil, herbs, and spices like coriander and cumin. The sauce is mainly popular in Tunisia (and, in fact, we attribute it to this country).

The next unforgettable meal on our trip through the Maghreb is Moroccan *tajine*. It's a meat (chicken, lamb, or mutton) or vegetable stew seasoned with various spices, from cinnamon to ginger, pepper, and saffron. It was traditional in pastoral societies, and was originally cooked in a terracotta pot that was buried among the embers of a fire. The shape of the pot evolved and came to resemble a double cone, which allows the steam to condense. To achieve the proper flavor, it's important for the pot to be made of terracotta and for the stew to cook a long time over low heat (preferably over burning embers).

Another experience not to be missed at a North African table is the long sequence of appetizers (*mezzes*, very popular in Egypt) that introduce the meal, a sign of appreciation for good flavors and the pleasure of conviviality. This is how *warah enab*, vine leaves stuffed with rice, is eaten. Shami, the classic flat bread, is used to scoop up exquisite vegetable dips like *foul*, made with fava beans, and *hummus*, made with chickpeas, or savory sauces like *dakka*, made with garlic, and *tahini*, made with sesame. All of these items are sampled between sips of Arak, an anise liqueur.

Heading south on our culinary voyage through Africa, the flavors become simpler and lighter as we reach tropical and equatorial climates with more humble agricultural traditions and less history of cultural exchange. However, it's very interesting to participate in a traditional lunch in the Horn of Africa, specifically in Ethiopia. Here you eat with your fingers, so a jug of water is brought to the table before the meal begins and everyone washes their hands. Then after an entrée of whey, you can try the national dish, *injera*. It's a spongy flatbread made of teff (a grain) and water. *Wot* is served on top, a chicken or mutton dish with a very spicy sauce made of red onion and *berberé*, a spice mix that deserves its own chapter. In the past, it was actually used as currency, and the main ingredient is hot red pepper, which is sweetened with cloves, cumin, garlic, ginger, pepper, cardamom, and other spices to taste. It's customary for the head of the household to begin by seasoning one side of the *injera*. Then everyone serves themselves, using three fingers of their right hand to dunk the bread in the sauces and scoop up pieces of meat. It's not unusual for the eaters to place a morsel directly in their neighbor's mouth as a sign of friendship.

Equatorial Africa presents us with a rather modest diet, where the more substantial dishes are chicken, mutton, and lamb (or fish in the coastal areas), which are usually grilled. These dishes tend to be served with rice, but there's another ingredient that we must taste while visiting the Gulf of Guinea: manioc. *Manihot esculenta*, also called tapioca or cassava, has been for Africa what the potato has been for Europe. And its history is similar, since it was first cultivated in South America. This particular tuber is like a hard, white carrot, and today it's the most important source of carbohydrates for the people of Central Africa. It's used for a thick paste called *fufu* in Cameroon, and for a type of *couscous* called *attékié* in the Ivory Coast.

The art of gastronomy takes on a bit more prestige in the Southern Hemisphere, where we've chosen dishes that are both flavorful and visually impressive, like chicken with piri piri sauce from Mozambique. The key ingredient here is the *piri piri* hot pepper, also called the "African devil", which was incorporated into Portuguese cuisine as well. Meanwhile, the recipe for Madagascan lobster blends typical Madagascan seafood with a tomato and ginger sauce on a bed of rice (long-grain white rice is fine, but if you can find it you can use *Rojomena*, the beautiful local red variety) that's cooked in coconut milk.

In South Africa you really could organize a vacation based on gastronomy alone. There you'll find a melting pot of culinary cultures that unites the indigenous Bantu, Xhosa, and Zulu traditions with Boer cuisine (from the first Dutch colonists) and Anglo-Saxon tastes. And you can travel from *pap* (a sort of maize porridge) served with hot *chakalaka* sauce, to *waterblommetije bredie*, a traditional Cape stew seasoned with water lilies, to *biltong*, strips of cured ostrich meat, and *koeksister*, braided doughnuts coated in syrup. There are two classic South African recipes in this collection: *bobotie*, a meatloaf with beef, curry, and apricot jam, and *sosatie* (from the Afrikaaner *sate*, "meat skewers", and *saus*, "hot sauce"), lamb skewers marinated overnight in onion, garlic, curry, hot red pepper, and tamarind paste. These dishes offer a complex harmony of flavors and an incredible blend of history and culture that enriches the gastronomic heritage of the entire continent.

LAMB TAJINE
WITH LEMON

MOROCCO

INGREDIENTS FOR 4 PEOPLE

3.3 LBS (1.5 KG) SHOULDER OR LEG OF LAMB,
  CUT INTO PIECES

2 1/2 CUPS (600 ML) BEEF BROTH

2 1/2 CUPS (430 G) CHICKPEAS

1.75 OZ (50 G) OLIVES

HALF A PRESERVED LEMON

HALF A FRESH LEMON

3 GARLIC CLOVES

2 ONIONS

1/3 CUP (80 ML) EXTRA-VIRGIN OLIVE OIL

3 TBSP FRESH CILANTRO, CHOPPED

1 TBSP GROUND GINGER

2 TSP GROUND CUMIN

1 TSP GROUND TURMERIC

1 TSP CINNAMON

1/2 TSP BLACK PEPPER

The word *tajine* refers to the pot that's used to cook this and similar dishes. It's a circular, two-piece, terracotta vessel, with a plate on the bottom and a conical cover on top that resembles an upside down funnel. This shape is responsible for perfectly cooked *tajine*, because the steam rises without escaping. Instead, it condenses and drifts back down over the meat, keeping it tender.

So when talking about *tajine* it's best to specify whether you mean the pot or the food. If you find yourself in Morocco or other North African countries and would like to buy a *tajine* pot, make sure it's one that can be used for cooking because many of those for sale are merely decorative.

Place the meat in a non-metallic bowl with the minced garlic, cumin, turmeric, ginger, cinnamon, pepper, and 2 tablespoons of oil. Let it marinate for 1 hour. In the meantime, slice the onion and prepare the broth. When the meat is done marinating, put it in a *tajine* or a large pan with the rest of the oil. Cook it on high heat, turning the pieces to make sure all sides are browned. As soon as they're browned, temporarily remove the meat from the pan. Cook the onion until it begins to brown, then return the meat to the pan. Add the broth, cover the pan, lower the heat, and let it simmer. Thoroughly rinse the peel of half a preserved lemon and cut it into strips. Then juice half a fresh lemon. After the *tajine* has simmered for an hour, add the lemon juice, lemon peel, olives, and chickpeas. Let it cook uncovered for about another 30 minutes. Add cilantro to taste before serving.

Preserving lemons is easy. You need fresh lemons, salt, black pepper or hot pepper, and olive oil. Wash the lemons and let them soak in water for three days, changing the water occasionally. Slice off the ends of the lemons, then slice them into quarters lengthwise, stopping the blade just before the cut goes all the way through. Each lemon should end up sliced into 4 wedges that are still attached at the base. Remove the seeds, rub the wedges with coarse salt, and "close" the lemons back up. Place them in a jar, adding a bit of salt between them. Fill the jar with oil and lemon juice (pure or diluted with boiling salted water). Season with pepper and keep in a cool, dark place. The lemons will be ready in a month.

KAAB EL GHAZAL

MOROCCO

INGREDIENTS FOR 4 PEOPLE

4 CUPS (500 G) FLOUR
2 3/4 CUPS (400 G) ALMONDS
2/3 CUP (150 G) SUGAR
1/4 CUP + 2 TBSP (100 G) BUTTER
3 TBSP ORANGE FLOWER WATER
1 EGG
POWDERED SUGAR (OR CRUSHED ALMONDS)
SALT

In French they're called *cornes de gazelle* ("gazelle horns"), a name that derives from the arched shape of these tempting and fragrant cookies.

Blanch the almonds and remove the skins. Grind them in a food processor along with the sugar, 3 1/2 tablespoons of butter melted in a double boiler, and 1 tablespoon of orange flower water. Blend well and shape the mixture into cylinders, about 2 1/3 inches long and wide as your finger. Melt the rest of the butter in a double boiler and combine with the flour, egg, a pinch of salt, 1 tablespoon of orange flower water, and 2 cups + 2 tablespoons of lukewarm water. Mix until a soft, elastic dough forms. Leave it to rest for 15 minutes, then roll it out to about 1/16 inch (1.5 mm) thick and cut it into 4-inch (10 cm) squares. Place a cylinder of the almond mix in the center of each dough square. Roll them diagonally and bend them into a "U" shape.
Preheat the oven to 325°F (170°C) and lay the rolled cookies in a buttered pan. Bake for 15 minutes.
While they're still hot, brush the *kaab el ghazal* with the remaining orange flower water and sprinkle with powdered sugar or crushed almonds.

These cookies are traditionally enjoyed with a cup of Moroccan tea, a green tea drink made with mint and sweetened with brown sugar.

CINNAMON BEGHRIR

MOROCCO

INGREDIENTS FOR 6 PEOPLE

1 1/2 CUPS (350 ML) MILK

2 CUPS (350 G) SEMOLINA

1 CUP + 3 TBSP (150 G) ALL-PURPOSE FLOUR

0.7 OZ (20 G) YEAST

3 EGGS

4 TBSP GROUND CINNAMON

POWDERED SUGAR

BABY MINT LEAVES

SALT

OIL

Beghrir are Moroccan pancakes characterized by their small size and soft, porous surface. Cinnamon beghrir make an excellent dessert and also work well for breakfast.

Sift together the flour and semolina in a large mixing bowl, and add a pinch of salt. Dissolve the yeast in 1 cup + 1 tablespoon (250 ml) of warm water and set aside.
Pour the milk into a small pot and add 1 cup + 1 tablespoon of water. Heat it, but don't let it boil. In the meantime, beat the eggs. Add them to the milk, stir well, and add half the liquid to the flour mixture. Add the water with dissolved yeast and mix well for about 10 minutes (there should be no lumps). Then add the rest of the liquid. Cover the dough with a towel and let it rest for at least 30 minutes.
When enough time has passed, oil the bottom of a nonstick pan and place it on the stove. When it's hot, pour in a ladleful of batter and distribute it evenly over the pan; each *beghrir* should be about 4 3/4 inches (12 cm) across and just under 1/8 inch (3 mm) thick. Cook on low heat until the batter sets and the surface looks spongy. Flip the *beghrir* and cook the other side. Remove it from the pan and place it with the fluffier side down on a slightly moistened towel.
Repeat the process until the batter is finished. Let the pancakes cool and sprinkle them with cinnamon, sugar, and baby mint leaves. Serve with mint tea.

You can reverse the amounts of flour and semolina in this recipe. You can also flavor the beghrir *with honey syrup instead of cinnamon and sugar. To make the syrup, boil a little bit of water in a small pot and add 4 tablespoons of honey. Let it boil for a few minutes, then drizzle it over the pancakes. You can even replace the water with 3 1/2 tablespoons (50g) of melted butter and caramelize the* beghrir *in the oven.*

MUTTON COUSCOUS
ALGERIA

INGREDIENTS FOR 4/6 PEOPLE

1 3/4 LBS (800 G) MUTTON	1 BUNCH OF PARSLEY
2 1/3 CUPS (420 G) COUS COUS	1 CELERY STALK
3.5 OZ (100 G) CHICKPEAS, ABOUT 1/2 CUP	1 POTATOES
1.76 OZ (50 G) RAISINS, ABOUT 1/3 CUP	3 TBSP EXTRA-VIRGIN OLIVE OIL
3 TBSP (40 G) BUTTER	1 TBSP BUTTER
3 ZUCCHINI	1 TSP GROUND HOT RED PEPPER
2 ONIONS	1/4 TSP SAFFRON
2 CARROTS	SALT
1 BUNCH OF CILANTRO	PEPPER

Couscous is the most traditional Maghreb dish, made from semolina and wheat flour. It was apparently invented by the Berbers before the Arab domination. In Morocco, it's served mainly with lighter meats, while in Algeria and Tunisia it's served with more savory stews, such as mutton. Homemade *couscous* is simple, but it requires a lot of time and experience. It also requires a particular pot, the *couscoussiére*. Luckily it's very easy to find ready-made in stores.

Rinse the chickpeas and soak them in cold water for 1 day. Just before straining them, dice the meat and mince the onion. Also slice the carrots, peel and cube the potatoes, and break up the celery stalk.
Put the meat in a pot with the carrots, chickpeas, onion, celery, potato, hot red pepper, and saffron. Sprinkle with pepper and pour in enough water to cover everything. Cook on low heat for 1 hour and season with salt. In the meantime, rinse the raisins and reconstitute them in warm water. Slice the zucchini into rounds, and chop the parsley and cilantro.
When 1 hour has passed, add those last few ingredients and cook for another 30 minutes, still on low heat.
When the stew is nearly done, boil 2 1/2 cups (600 ml) of water in a small pot. Put the *couscous* in another pot (don't turn on the heat), break it up well with a fork, and slowly add the oil. Don't let any lumps form. Pour the boiling water over the couscous and let it sit for 5 - 6 minutes until all the water is absorbed. Fluff with a fork and put the heat on the lowest setting. Add the butter in small flakes and stir well to combine. Transfer the *couscous* to a serving platter. Arrange the meat and vegetables on the *couscous*, pour some of the broth they cooked in over it, and serve. It's usually accompanied by a bowl of *harissa*.

Other vegetables can be added to mutton couscous, particularly fresh broad beans and sliced tomatoes, which should be added to the pot with the zucchini. The dish can also be seasoned with fennel seeds, cayenne pepper, and other spices.

HARISSA
TUNISIA

INGREDIENTS FOR 6 PEOPLE
7 OZ (200 G) FRESH RED CHILI PEPPERS,
    ABOUT 4 1/2 PEPPERS
4 GARLIC CLOVES
2 TBSP CORIANDER SEEDS
1 TBSP DRIED MINT LEAVES
1 TBSP FINE SALT
1 TBSP CARAWAY SEEDS
CUMIN
EXTRA-VIRGIN OLIVE OIL

Spicy flavors are highly appreciated in the Maghreb, as evidenced by the popularity of *harissa*, a Tunisian hot pepper sauce (the name means "crushed"). It can also be purchased ready-made, but it's traditionally prepared at home. The original recipe is extremely spicy; consider substituting red bell peppers or tomatoes for some of the chili peppers.

Wash the chilies and remove the stems. Cut them lengthwise and remove the seeds, then soak them in a large bowl of cold water for at least 1 hour. Clean the garlic while they soak.
Traditionally the chili peppers, garlic, cumin, caraway, coriander, salt, and mint are combined in a mortar. The ingredients are then crushed with a pestle for a long time, adding oil until a dense sauce similar to tomato paste is formed. But to save time, you can bypass this ancient method with a food processor.
Let the *harissa* rest in a cool place for half a day before serving. If you don't eat it all right away, cover the surface with oil and store it in the refrigerator in a well-sealed container.

Caraway is a fragrant plant historically popular throughout North Africa, Europe, and the Middle East, but today it's cultivated in America as well. It's also called "Persian cumin" and resembles fennel. The seeds have a pungent flavor, midway between anise and cumin. They quickly lose their taste once they've been ground, so it's best to buy and keep them whole.

TUNA AND EGG BRIKS

TUNISIA

INGREDIENTS FOR 4 PEOPLE

4 SHEETS OF BRIK DOUGH (MALSOUKA)
4 OZ (113 G) TUNA, PACKED IN WATER
1 OZ (28 G) EDAM CHEESE
4 EGGS
1 BUNCH OF PARSLEY
1 TBSP BUTTER
1/2 TBSP CAPERS
OIL FOR FRYING

Briks (also *bricks*, *buriks*, or *buricks*) are fried turnovers. In Tunisia they're omnipresent, eaten as snacks, appetizers, side dishes, or entrées. The most common filling is a mix of egg, parsley, and tuna. The latter is sometimes replaced with minced beef, chicken, lamb, or mutton. In another popular version, half a minced onion is added as well.

Lay out the 4 sheets of *malsouka* dough on 4 slightly concave plates. Drain the tuna, put it in a bowl, and break it up with a fork. Divide it into four portions and place one in the center of each sheet of dough. Rinse and mince the capers and parsley, grate the cheese, and mix them all together. Spoon a quarter of the mixture onto each sheet of dough, then break an egg over each one.
Melt the butter and brush it around the edges of the dough. Fold each dough sheet in half, slightly rolling the edges to seal them.
Heat some oil into a frying pan. When the temperature is right, fry the first *brik*. Flip it after 2 minutes. When the other side has turned golden brown, remove it from the pan and place it on a plate lined with paper towels. Do the same with the other turnovers, then serve them hot with *harissa* sauce or a lemon wedge.

Malsouka is a type of phyllo dough that's difficult for the inexperienced to make at home, so buying it ready-made is recommended. You can find it at many Arabic butcher shops, North African and Middle Eastern grocery stores, and even some Indian grocery stores.

MAKROUD

TUNISIA

INGREDIENTS FOR 4 PEOPLE

3 CUPS (600 G) SUGAR

1 1/2 CUPS (250 G) SEMOLINA

3.5 OZ (100 G) DATES, ABOUT 1/2 CUP CHOPPED

2/3 CUP (150 ML) EXTRA-VIRGIN OLIVE OIL
   (OR CLARIFIED BUTTER)

1 LEMON

OIL FOR FRYING

BAKING SODA

GROUND CINNAMON

SALT

Makroud are pastries made with dates, a particularly nutritious fruit that plays a large role in North African cooking.

Heat the olive oil in a double boiler and pour the semolina into a bowl with a pinch of baking powder When the oil is lukewarm, set aside 1 tablespoon and pour the rest over the semolina. Add salt to taste and start mixing with your hands, softening the semolina a bit with 2/3 cup of hot (not boiling) water. Continue mixing until a dense dough forms. Let it cool, then work the dough for a few more minutes. Cover it with a towel and let it rest for about 30 minutes.
Pit the dates and chop them into small pieces (you can also run them through a food mill). Sprinkle them with a pinch of cinnamon, then add 1/2 cup of sugar and the remaining tablespoon of oil. Combine well and form the resulting mixture into small cylinders as wide as your finger.
Roll the dough out on a pastry board, to a thickness of about 1/2 inch (1.5 cm). Cut it into strips about 4 inches (10 cm) wide. Place a cylinder of the date mixture lengthwise on each strip of dough. Roll them up so the dates are covered and then gently flatten them. Continue until you run out of dates and dough. Decorate the filled dough strips by carving geometric patterns with a knife and then cut them into little 2-inch (5 cm) squares.
Fry the *makroud* in a large pan and let them cool on a plate covered with paper towels.
While they cool, squeeze the lemon into a small pot and add 2/3 cup of water. Heat it, then add the rest of the sugar and stir until a sort of syrup has formed. Dip the cookies in one by one letting the excess syrup drip off, and serve.

Makroud *are very high in calories, but you can make a lighter version. Don't add any sugar to the dates and bake the* makroud *(20 minutes at 400°F/200°C) instead of frying them.*

SHARBA

LIBYA

INGREDIENTS FOR 4 PEOPLE

1/2 LB (225 G) LAMB
1/2 CUP (70 G) BARLEY
2 - 3 TOMATOES
1 LEMON
1 BUNCH OF PARSLEY (OR CILANTRO)
1 LARGE ONION

4 TBSP CLARIFIED BUTTER (OR OIL)
1 TBSP TOMATO PASTE
1 TSP *HARARAT*
HOT RED PEPPER
DRIED MINT LEAVES
SALT

Sharba is a Libyan soup made with lamb and barley. The following is the traditional recipe, which calls for the addition of spices and few other ingredients. There are versions that include carrots or other vegetables, and following the arrival of Italian colonists, it became common in some parts of Libya to use pasta instead of barley.

Chop the lamb into small pieces, juice the lemon, dice the tomatoes, and mince the parsley and onion. Sauté the onion in a pot with the clarified butter for a few seconds, then add the lamb. Brown it on medium heat, adding the parsley, *hararat*, tomatoes, a pinch of hot red pepper, and the tomato paste. When the meat is fully browned, add just enough water to cover it. Reduce the heat to the lowest setting and simmer for about 30 minutes. Then add the barley along with more water, and bring it to a boil. Reduce the heat again and cook for a little over 10 minutes. When it's just about done, add a pinch a salt and the lemon juice (if you don't care much for the flavor, you can add just half). Serve with a garnish of dried mint leaves.

Hararat *(or* hrarat) *is a very common spice mix in Libya. There's no official recipe for it; the types and amounts of individual spices can vary quite drastically. The main ingredients are always cinnamon, cilantro, pepper and/or hot red pepper. But you can also find cumin, nutmeg, ginger, turmeric, and many others in the mix.*

FUL MUDAMMAS
EGYPT

Difficulty: Easy - Time: 2 hours e 45 minutes + soaking and resting time

INGREDIENTS FOR 4 PEOPLE

1 1/3 LBS (600 G) DRY HORSE BEANS OR FAVA BEANS

4 GARLIC CLOVES

2 EGGS

2 LEMONS

1 SPRING ONION

EXTRA-VIRGIN OLIVE OIL

PARSLEY

CUMIN

GROUND HOT RED PEPPER

SALT

PEPPER

The origins of this tasty broad bean soup are unclear. Coptic Orthodox Christians, mainly in Egypt, Ethiopia, and Eritrea, believe that their ancestors invented it in the first few centuries A.D. But according to Egyptian tradition, the dish was already known in the time of the pharaohs.

Rinse the beans thoroughly under running water, then soak them in cold water for at least 12 hours. Strain them, rinse them, and drain them well. Transfer the beans to a pot and cover them with water, lightly salted. Simmer on low heat for about 2 1/2 hours (check to make sure they're tender), stirring occasionally. Meanwhile hard boil the eggs, remove the shells, and cut them into wedges. Juice the lemons and crush the garlic.

Strain the beans when they're done. Season with the garlic and lemon juice, then let them sit for 15 minutes. Take this time to mince the parsley and spring onion, then mix them with 1 tablespoon of oil and a pinch of salt to taste. Add it all to the beans and serve them still hot. Serve the eggs separately. Each diner can add cumin, pepper, and/or hot red pepper according to personal preference.

Horse beans (the scientific name is vicia faba equina*) are a type of broad bean with medium-sized flat seeds, each weighing about 0.035 ounces (1 g). In Europe they were used mainly as horse feed for a long time, and their gastronomic value has only recently been reconsidered thanks to the influence of North African cuisine. The* ful mudammas *recipe can also be made with the same amount of tick beans (*vicia faba minor*), which are smaller and darker than horse beans, or with easier to find fava beans.*

HUMMUS

EGYPT

INGREDIENTS FOR 4 PEOPLE

2/3 LB (300 G) DRY CHICKPEAS (NOT TOO MATURE),
    ABOUT 1 1/2 CUPS
1 LEMON
1 GARLIC CLOVE
1 RED HOT CHILI PEPPER
3 TBSP EXTRA-VIRGIN OLIVE OIL
2 TBSP PARSLEY
1 TBSP CUMIN SEEDS
SALT

Hummus can be served as an appetizer, or as a topping for bread, vegetables, and other heavier fare. This icon of Egyptian and Middle Eastern cuisine is both healthy and easy to make. It's also very tasty thanks to the delicate flavor of chickpeas, combined with the tartness of lemon juice and tempered by the aroma of garlic.

Rinse the chickpeas in running water, then soak them in a bowl of cold water for 1 day. Strain the chickpeas and rinse them again.
Peel and crush the garlic, then heat it in a pot with 2 tablespoons of oil. Before it starts to brown, add the chickpeas and pour in enough water to cover them. Cover the pot and cook for at least 2 hours. In the meantime, juice the lemon and mince the chili pepper and parsley.
After 2 hours, check to make sure the chickpeas have softened (if not, let them cook longer). Strain them and save 2/3 cup of the water they cooked in.
Mash the chickpeas and stir them with a wooden spoon until they reach a soft, creamy texture (you can also put them in a food processor). If necessary, add some of the water you saved to soften the mixture. Add the cumin, lemon juice, and a pinch of salt. Mix thoroughly and transfer to a serving plate. Drizzle with 1 tablespoon of oil, sprinkle with parsley and hot red pepper, and serve.

The most common variation of this recipe concerns the addition of cumin and hot pepper. Rather than adding them after you crush the chickpeas, you can put them all in the pot with the garlic and toast them for 2 minutes before adding the legumes. However, you should use ground hot red pepper instead of a fresh minced chili in this case. In another variation, 1 heaping tablespoon of tahini (sesame paste) is added just before mashing the chickpeas.

WARAH ENAB
EGYPT

INGREDIENTS FOR 6 PEOPLE

1 LB (450 G) FRESH VINE LEAVES

1 CUP (200 G) BASMATI RICE

1/3 CUP (50 G) PINE NUTS

2 - 3 TOMATOES

1 ONION

1 LEMON

4 GARLIC CLOVES

3 TBSP EXTRA-VIRGIN OLIVE OIL

2 TBSP PARSLEY, CHOPPED

DRY MINT LEAVES

NUTMEG

GROUND CINNAMON

SALT

PEPPER

Warah (or *warak*) *enab* are vine leaves stuffed with seasoned rice. It's not clear whether they're of Egyptian or Libyan origin, but what's certain is that they're popular today throughout the Middle East and beyond, especially in Greece.

Blanch the vine leaves in salted water to soften them, and remove the stems. Rinse the rice in cold water and let it soak for 10 minutes. Meanwhile crumble a few mint leaves and mince the pine nuts and onion. Peel the tomato, remove the seeds, and dice it.

Strain the rice and transfer it to a large bowl. Add the pine nuts, mint, onion, tomato, parsley, oil, and a pinch of cinnamon and nutmeg. Season with salt and pepper to taste and stir until well-blended; this will be the filling.

Select the largest vine leaves and lay them on a table with the rough side up. Place a spoonful of filling a little above the base of each leaf and use your fingers to spread it. Fold over the base and sides of the leaf, roll it up, and gently flatten it.

When you're done, line the bottom of a large pot with discarded vine leaves. Lay the stuffed leaves inside, one next to the other, positioning them so they don't open. Peel the garlic cloves and tuck them among the leaves. Juice the lemon and pour the juice into the pot, then add 2/3 cup (160 ml) of water. To keep the rolled leaves still, place a flat terracotta or glass plate over them. Gently press it down and leave it there while they cook. Cover the pot and cook on low heat for 40-45 minutes. Add more water if necessary.

Serve hot or cold on a bed of vine leaves, and garnish with lemon slices.

If you don't have a large enough pot, you can place the warah enab *in two layers. Be careful to lay them perpendicular to each other (each layer should be placed in the opposite direction of the previous layer). If you don't have enough "throwaway" vine leaves, you can line the bottom of the pot with an even layer of stewed carrots sliced into rounds.*

CHICKEN YASSA
SENEGAL

Difficulty: Medium - Time: 1 hour 15 minutes + marinating time

INGREDIENTS FOR 4 PEOPLE

3 LBS (1.4 KG) CHICKEN, CUT INTO PIECES
8 WHITE ONIONS
4 GARLIC CLOVES
3 LIMES
2 TBSP MUSTARD

1 TSP CRUSHED RED PEPPER
BAY LEAVES
PEANUT OIL
SALT
PEPPER

Yassa is a lime-based (or lemon-based) marinade that was once used to tenderize lesser cuts of meat. Today it's mainly appreciated for the aroma it lends to fish and meat, especially chicken.

Squeeze the lime into a bowl with two or three torn bay leaves, 1 tablespoon of mustard, and the crushed red pepper. Season with salt and pepper to taste and mix thoroughly. Rinse the chicken pieces under running water and pat them dry. Let the chicken marinate in the lime mixture for at least 2 hours (in Senegal the marinating can last an entire day).
Preheat the oven to 325°F (170°C). Remove the chicken from the marinade and drain off any excess. Set the marinade aside for later. Bake the chicken in a pan lined with aluminum foil for a little more than 20 minutes. As an alternative, you can also brown the chicken pieces in a saucepan with a bit of oil.
Meanwhile, peel the garlic and cut the onions into relatively thick slices.
Once you've taken the chicken out of the oven, sauté the garlic and onions in a large pan with bit of peanut oil, adding a pinch of pepper and the rest of the mustard. When the onions have softened, add the chicken along with the juices from the pan and the marinade you set aside earlier. Cook on medium-low heat for 30 minutes, checking every now and then to make sure the chicken doesn't stick to the bottom of the pan. If it does, add a little water.

White rice is the ideal side dish for yassa. Boil 2 cups + 2 tablespoons of water with 2 cups (400 g) of rice until all the liquid is absorbed, which should only take a few minutes. In the meantime, boil a little bit of water in a large pot. Pour the rice into a strainer and place it over the large pot so that it doesn't touch the water. Cover and cook for another 15 - 20 minutes.

MAFE

GAMBIA

INGREDIENTS FOR 6 PEOPLE

6 CUPS (1.5 L) VEGETABLE BROTH
   OR LIGHT BEEF BROTH
2 LBS (900 G) LAMB (OR VEAL)
3/4 CUP (200 G) PEANUT BUTTER
3 - 4 TBSP PEANUT OIL
3 TBSP TOMATO PURÉE
2 ONIONS
2 POTATOES

2 SWEET POTATOES (OR 1 LARGE YAM)
2 CARROTS
2 AFRICAN RED HOT PEPPERS
2 GARLIC CLOVES
1 CELERY STALK
BAY LEAVES
SALT
PEPPER

The Republic of The Gambia is a relatively small country, completely surrounded by Senegal. Gambian cuisine doesn't differ much from its neighboring country, and one of the most popular dishes they share is *mafe* (or *mafè*), a beef stew made with peanut butter.

Heat the broth, and mince one clove of garlic and an onion. Chop the lamb, then peel the carrots and all the potatoes (if they're large, roughly chop them into smaller pieces). Dilute the tomato purée with 1/3 cup of water or broth.
Heat the peanut oil in a large pan and start browning the meat on medium heat. After a few seconds, add the minced garlic and onion. Wait 2 more minutes, then add the tomato purée and all the broth.
Mince the other onion and garlic clove. As soon as the broth starts to boil, add them to the pot along with the hot peppers (be careful not to break them or the *mafe* could be too spicy). Melt the peanut butter in 2/3 cup of hot water and add it to the pot, stirring well. Add the carrots, potatoes, celery, and a couple of bay leaves.
Bring it back to a boil and let it cook, stirring frequently to keep the peanut butter from sinking to the bottom and sticking. Turn the heat off when nearly all the broth has evaporated. Season with salt and pepper to taste, and serve with a plate of Thai rice.

The recipe for mafe *is very adaptable, especially when it comes to the vegetables. You can also add a chopped turnip and cabbage, a whole head of garlic, and a couple of* bamies, *a vegetable similar to zucchini.*

INJERA

ETHIOPIA

Difficulty: Easy - Time: 40 minutes + resting time

INGREDIENTS FOR 4/6 PEOPLE
3 3/4 CUPS (450 G) ALL-PURPOSE FLOUR
2 CUPS (300 G) CORNMEAL
1 1/2 CUPS (250 G) SEMOLINA
0.7 OZ (20 G) YEAST
1/4 TSP BAKING SODA

Almost all Ethiopian and Eritrean specialties are served on a bed of *injera* (or *enjera*), a soft, spongy, flat bread that serves as both a base and a side dish for meat and vegetable dishes.
 It's traditionally made with *teff* flour, a typical grain from the Horn of Africa. Its main nutritional attribute is its lack of gluten and notably high levels of iron, calcium, and other minerals. Unfortunately, it's difficult to find *teff* flour, so it can be substituted with millet, or a mix of cornmeal, semolina, and wheat flour, as shown in the following recipe.

Sift together the semolina, flour, and cornmeal in a large mixing bowl (or onto a pastry board). Dissolve the yeast in 1 cup (250 ml) of warm water (about 113°F/45°C). Slowly add the dissolved yeast to the flours, and mix well. Gradually add 1 more cup (250 ml) of warm water. When everything is well combined, transfer it to a large, deep bowl. Cover it with a towel and let it rise in a cool place for at least 1 day.
Mix the risen dough, working in the baking soda, then slowly add enough warm water to turn the dough into a liquid batter.
Heat a heavy-bottomed nonstick pan that's just slightly wider than a plate. Pour in a bit of the batter, forming a layer about 1/8 inch (3 - 4 mm) thick. Cover the pan as soon as the batter begins to set, and cook for 2 - 3 minutes on that same side (it doesn't need to brown). Remove the *injera* from the pan and place it on a cloth. Continue until all the batter is finished, making sure not to put any *injera* directly on top of each other. Let them cool and serve.

You can use more water at the beginning (at least 4 cups/1 L) instead of adding more water after the dough has risen. In this case, mix the dough just enough to incorporate the baking soda once it's risen, and make sure the dough is liquid enough to be poured into the pan. If it isn't you will have to add more warm water.

MUTZI WA SAMAKI

KENYA

INGREDIENTS FOR 4 PEOPLE

3 LBS (1.4 KG) PERCH FILLETS

1 3/4 CUPS (375 ML) COCONUT MILK

5 - 6 GARLIC CLOVES

1 BELL PEPPER

1 HOT RED PEPPER

1 ONION

3 TOMATOES

2 TBSP TAMARIND PASTE (OR LEMON JUICE)

3 TBSP VEGETABLE OIL

3 TBSP *GARAM MASALA* (A HOT SPICE BLEND)

SALT

PEPPER

Mutzi wa samaki is fish cooked in coconut milk and hot spices. The recipe is popular in Kenya, Uganda, and Tanzania. It derives from a recipe that Indian merchants introduced to the people of Zanzibar. In fact, the archipelago had long been a point of contact between Asian and East African culture and gastronomy.

Rinse and dry the fish fillets. If they're very large, cut them into roughly 1/2 pound (225 g) pieces. Remove the seeds from the bell pepper and chop it finely. Slice or dice the tomatoes and chop up the hot pepper. Peel and mince the onion and garlic.
Pour the vegetable oil into a large skillet and set it on high heat. Briefly sear the fish on both sides, then remove it from the pan. Let it drain and set it aside.
Reduce the heat and sauté the onion in the same oil. After 1 minute, add the garlic, hot pepper, and a sprinkling of pepper. Wait another 2 minutes, then add the bell pepper and tomatoes. Mix well, then shortly after add the coconut milk, *garam masala*, tamarind paste (or lemon juice), and salt to taste.
As soon as the sauce starts to simmer, add the fish and cover the pan. Let it cook on medium heat for 8 - 10 minutes, then serve with boiled rice or unleavened bread.

In southwestern Kenya, on the Tanzanian and Ugandan border, mtuzi wa samaki *is made with freshwater fish from Lake Victoria. Saltwater fish are used in Zanzibar and on the coasts. The perch fillets used here can be easily replaced with other types of fish. You also can't find the same vegetables in all the different areas where* mtuzi wa samaki *is popular, and one of the more common variations calls for a little bit of spinach. Finally, if you can't find the garam masala, you can use more hot pepper and other spices.*

MEAT AND PUMPKIN STEW

TANZANIA

INGREDIENTS FOR 4 PEOPLE

1.3 LBS (600 G) LAMB (SHOULDER IS BEST)

2/3 LB (300 G) PUMPKIN,
   A LITTLE OVER 2 1/2 CUPS CUBED

3 TBSP (45 G) CLARIFIED BUTTER

3 LARGE RIPE TOMATOES

3 GARLIC CLOVES, MINCED

2 SMALL ONIONS

1 GREEN CHILI PEPPER, MINCED

1 SMALL PIECE OF FRESH GINGER

SALT

PEPPER

When animals are raised mainly for their milk, as they traditionally are in Tanzania, they're generally slaughtered at an advanced age. Making a stew is the best way to cook the meat, which would otherwise be too tough. This beef and pumpkin stew came to be for that very reason. Mutton or beef were usually used, but the dish is best with lamb shoulder.

Dice the meat and pumpkin, and mince the chili pepper. Peel and chop the garlic and tomatoes, slice the onions, and grate the ginger.
Heat half the butter in a saucepan and sauté the lamb, seasoning with salt and pepper to taste. When the meat starts to brown on all sides, turn off the heat and set it aside.
In another pot sauté the garlic, onion, tomato, chili pepper, and ginger with the rest of the butter. After about 8 minutes, add the meat. Let it all cook together for a few minutes, mixing well. Add 1/2 cup (120 ml) of water, cover the pot, and cook for 30 minutes. Then add the pumpkin with 1 cup (250 ml) of water, and cover again. Cooking time will vary depending on how large the pieces of meat are, but on average, it should take another 30 minutes on medium-low heat. If the stew gets too dry, add more water.
Serve it hot with boiled rice.

For a particularly colorful table presentation, you can hollow out a medium-sized pumpkin, remove the top, and fill it with stew.

GRILLED CHICKEN WITH PIRI PIRI SAUCE

MOZAMBIQUE

INGREDIENTS FOR 4 PEOPLE

2 LBS (900 G) CHICKEN, CUT INTO PIECES

3 *PIRI PIRI* PEPPERS (OR ANOTHER VERY
   SPICY VARIETY)

2 GARLIC CLOVES

1 LEMON

1 RED BELL PEPPER

4 TBSP EXTRA-VIRGIN OLIVE OIL

1 TSP SALT

Grilled chicken with *piri piri* is of Portuguese origin. It's a big favorite in Mozambique and South Africa, both countries colonized by Portugal. For those who aren't used to the strong flavors, the sauce might be too spicy. *Piri piri* (also called *African devil*) is in fact one of the most "aggressive" hot peppers in Africa. Therefore, the following recipe substitutes a red bell pepper for two of the hot peppers in the original recipe.

Grill the bell pepper, peel it, and remove the seeds. Peel and crush the garlic, finely chop the hot peppers, and juice the lemon. Combine the oil and lemon in a large bowl and mix well. Add the salt, chili pepper, and minced bell pepper. Mix it all together (you can save time by using a food processor) and let it sit for a few minutes. Take this time to rinse the chicken pieces and gently pat them dry.
Cover the chicken with the sauce and let it marinate in a cool place for 2 hours. Meanwhile light the grill, preferably using wood with no chemical additives.
Grill the chicken over low flames for 10 - 15 minutes, turning it over several times and basting it with the marinade. Cooking time may vary depending on the size of the chicken pieces. If there's any leftover marinade, heat it in a small pan, perhaps with another tablespoon of oil, and bring it to the table with the chicken. Serve with salad and cooked vegetables.

If you don't have a grill, you can bake the chicken at 400°F (200°C). Average cooking time is 50 minutes, but it can vary considerably depending on the size of the chicken pieces. If you chose to bake it, you should still baste the chicken with the marinade occasionally.

BOBOTIE

SOUTH AFRICA

INGREDIENTS FOR 4 PEOPLE

4 1/4 CUPS (1000 ML) MILK

1.1 LBS (500 G) LAMB, CUT INTO PIECES

1 2/3 CUPS (100 G) FRESH BREADCRUMBS

3 1/2 TBSP (50 G) BUTTER

1/2 CUP (50 G) SULTANAS (GOLDEN RAISINS)

12 ALMONDS

2 EGGS

2 ONIONS

1 APPLE

1 TBSP SUGAR

1 TBSP *MASALA* (CURRY POWDER)

1 TBSP WINE VINEGAR

1 TSP GROUND SAFFRON

BAY LEAVES

SALT

PEPPER

Bobotie is a South African dish made from ground meat, eggs, milk, and spices. It dates back to the 17th century when Dutch colonists at the Cape of Good Hope tried to recreate a dish from Indonesia, one of their other colonies. The recipe was significantly modified and adapted, but the name still evokes *bobotok*, a well-known Indonesian dish made with coconut milk. However, *bobotie* is made with cow's milk.

Wash the raisins. Chop the almonds into small pieces. Put the fresh breadcrumbs in a bowl with 1 cup + 2 tablespoons of milk. Use a fork to press them down into the milk until they've softened. Peel and slice the onions, then brown them slightly in the butter. Transfer them to a large bowl and add the meat, breadcrumbs with milk, raisins, almonds, sugar, saffron, curry powder, and vinegar. Peel and slice the apple, then add that as well. Mix it all together and add a couple of bay leaves.

Transfer it to a greased pan and cook for 1 hour on medium-low heat. Then break the eggs into a bowl with 1 cup + 2 tablespoons of milk. Add salt and pepper to taste. Beat it well with a fork and add it to the *bobotie*. Cook for at least another 20 minutes, then transfer to a platter and serve with white rice.

Today bobotie *is popular throughout Africa and the recipe has generated dozens of variations, particularly concerning the amount of milk and the type of meat (using beef or mutton instead of lamb). The almonds are sometimes substituted with 2/3 cup of blueberries or a few tablespoons of jelly are used instead of the apple.*

SOSATIE

SOUTH AFRICA

Difficulty: Easy · Time: 30 minutes + marinating and soaking time

INGREDIENTS FOR 4 PEOPLE

1.3 LBS (600 G) LAMB

1 3/4 CUPS (250 G) DRIED APRICOTS

2 ONIONS

2 GARLIC CLOVES

1 TBSP MASALA (CURRY POWDER)

1 TBSP BROWN SUGAR

1 TBSP WHITE WINE VINEGAR

CORNSTARCH

SALT

PEPPER

One of the main features of South African cuisine is the fusion of sweet and savory, especially meat and fruit. It's exemplified in the recipe for *sosaties*, grilled skewers of lamb or mutton with dried fruit.

Cut the lamb into 1-inch cubes (2.5 cm) and set it aside. Mince the garlic and cut the onions into wedges. Combine them with the curry powder, sugar, cornstarch, and vinegar in a large bowl. Heat the mixture in a pan for a few minutes and return it to the bowl. Add the lamb and let it marinate for half a day in a cool place (or in the refrigerator).
When enough time has passed, soak the dried apricots in hot water for about 30 minutes. Then skewer them, alternating with chunks of lamb. Save the marinade and use it to baste the *sosaties* while they cook. Grill the skewers for 10 minutes, seasoning with salt and pepper.

One of the numerous versions of this recipe calls for just over 1 cup (150g) of dried apricots. To make up for the rest, 2 tablespoons of apricot preserves are added to the marinade. Other ingredients can also be added to the marinade, such as 1 tablespoon of tamarind juice or sherry, and a pinch of hot red pepper.

MADAGASCAN LOBSTER WITH RICE

MADAGASCAR

INGREDIENTS FOR 4 PEOPLE

2 LIVE LOBSTERS, ABOUT 1 3/4 LBS (800 G) EACH

2 1/3 CUPS (450 G) BASMATI OR THAI RICE

1 3/4 CUPS (400 ML) COCONUT MILK

4 LARGE RIPE TOMATOES

2 GARLIC CLOVES

1 ONION

1 SMALL PIECE OF FRESH GINGER

2 TBSP EXTRA-VIRGIN OLIVE OIL

Madagascan cuisine is heavily influenced by Indian cuisine, especially when it comes to rice and single-course meals. Meats (chicken, zebu, or pork) are most prominent in the inland areas, while the coastal gastronomic traditions concentrate on fish, especially shellfish. As this recipe demonstrates, lobster is in the lead among the latter. Of course, the original recipe calls for lobster from the Indian Ocean, but other varieties will work just fine.

Bring a large pot of water to a boil. Peel and mince the garlic and onion. Peel and chop the tomatoes, and grate the ginger.

Stretch out the lobsters' tails and insert wooden skewers to keep them straight. Immerse them in the boiling water and cover the pot. Cook for about 10 minutes (15 minutes if they weigh over 2.2 lbs/1 kg). Take them out of the water and remove the meat through a lengthwise cut down the center. Try to keep both halves of the shell intact because you will use them later to present the finished dish.

Rinse and strain the rice, then heat it in a pot with the coconut milk. When the milk starts to boil, reduce the heat to the lowest setting. From this point the rice should cook for 15 minutes. If the milk is evaporating too quickly, add a bit of water.

Pour the oil into a saucepan with the garlic, onion, ginger, and tomatoes. Cook on low heat for 10 minutes, making sure nothing sticks to the pan. Add the lobster meat, stir for another 5 minutes, and turn off the heat.

Divide the rice onto 4 plates, and pour a spoonful of the lobster and tomato sauce over each one. Then place half a shell on top, fill it with the rest of the sauce, and serve.

Choose 2 female lobsters if possible, because their meat is more concentrated. You can recognize the females by the double swimmerets under their tails, which are used to carry eggs.

ASIA

It might seem unusual to introduce Asian gastronomy with a recipe as Yiddish-sounding as gefilte fish. Yet there is no recipe more representative of Jewish culinary traditions. Since large numbers of Ashkenazi Jews began immigrating to Palestine from Central Europe as a result of growing Nazism in the 1930s, and continued to do so in the post-war period, this "filled fish" has become the official dish of Jerusalem and surrounding areas. However, the translation "filled fish" is not quite accurate. Called *dagim memula'im* in Hebrew, gefilte fish is more like a "fish loaf" or fish patties, made from various types of deboned fish (originally carp, pike, or mullet) combined with onions, carrots, and hard-boiled eggs. It's a classic holiday dish that can be prepared the day before and eaten cold so there's no need to clean the fish on the holiday, which would violate Shabbat rules. It's fascinating to think of this recipe as a sort of bridge that spans two continents, a bridge built by a nomadic population in honor of their religion, bearing all the weight of its symbolism and historic contradictions.

Now that we've finally set foot in the continent of Asia by way of fish, we face a gastronomic reality that's difficult to wade through. Asia is an immense territory with thousands of cultural groups and even more culinary traditions. There we find populations of wandering herders and warriors, builders of empires and imperial kitchens, residents of long lost glacial villages, and developers of ancient survival techniques. With a quick division of the map and a great deal of simplification, we can split the continent into two sections: areas where people eat with their hands, and areas where people eat with chopsticks. We can put the entire Middle East in the first category, along with South Asia and Indonesia. East Asia and Mainland Southeast Asia are in the second category (we can liken the popularity of forks and knives in those regions to the fusion food trend and use of chopsticks in the West—both are examples of globalization, more or less imposed).

Let's start with the basics, that is, with our hands. This is the tradition among the pastoral societies that developed from the Middle Eastern

FROM FINGERS TO CHOPSTICKS

deserts to the Karakoram mountain range. The use of fingers for picking up food was refined over the centuries with the aid of a "utensil" that was important not only on a technical level but also in terms of nutrition—bread. Unleavened bread was wide and flat, making it easy to tear into strips and scoop up sauces and other hot foods without burning your hands. Such breads crop up in many languages: *yufka* in Turkish, *markouk* in Arabic (from the dome-shaped oven used to cook it), saj in Lebanese, *pita* (perhaps an ancestor of Italian pizza?) throughout the Mediterranean, and *roti*, *poli*, *phulka*, or *kulcha* in India. Aside from a few variations in flour composition and cooking method, it's the same basic bread, flat and often unsalted. It lends itself to quick preparation and cooking because it doesn't need to rise, which makes it ideal for outdoor living and early morning departures. The best description of an ancient shepherd's meal is in Exodus 12, which tells of how the Israelites fled Egypt. They ate unleavened bread and lamb, which had to be roasted, "not boiled in water". According to the Bible, boiling would have cost too much time. "In this manner you shall eat it: with your belt fastened, your sandals on your feet, and your staff in your hand"—ready to leave at any moment.

In this collection you will find unleavened bread under its most popular South Asian name, *chapati*. We attribute it to Pakistan because the most ancient cooking method for this bread (laid over a flat rock heated by fire) originated in the valleys between the Karakoram and the Hindu Kush. It's usually spread with *ghee* (clarified butter) and served with *dal* (lentil soup), but it's also ideal for scooping up meat stews like Indian lamb curry. The Armenian version of the *kebab* includes another type of flat bread with a lamb and feta topping. The Turkish *kebab*, the best-known version in the world, is a true "on-the-go" sandwich that consists of bread wrapped around a filling of thinly sliced beef or mutton with onion, cucumber, and hot sauces.

There is a clear divide in the path of gastronomic evolution beyond the phase of people eating with their hands or with the help of bread. Fingers were artificially extended through the use of knives and forks (the Western path) or chopsticks, which represent the second geographical category of Asia. The mark of great empires throughout ancient history (Chinese dynasties, the Land of the Rising Sun, the kingdoms of Mainland Southeast Asia), they symbolize royal kitchens and complex etiquette. If there is one element that sums up the great cultural divide between East and West, it is indeed chopsticks, not just because of the manual dexterity they require (even after years of practice, Westerners struggle to wield a pair chopsticks as well as a Chinese preschooler) but for the products, recipes, and cooking and serving methods associated with them. Chopsticks are ancient utensils much older than the fork, which has only been documented since the High Middle Ages in Europe. Iron chopsticks were discovered in a tomb in central China that dates back to the Shang-Yin dynasty, which began in the 17th century BC, and it's likely that they had already been used for centuries prior to that (though made of different materials). One of the legends surrounding their origin refers to Daji, the emperor's concubine, who took the jade hairpins out of her hair and used them to feed the emperor when his food was too hot. Another legend tells the story of the hero Da Yu, the "Tamer of the Flood". He needed to return to his difficult task quickly and couldn't wait for his food to cool, so he used two tree branches to grab pieces of boiling hot meat from the pot.

Whether they were made of jade, wood, iron, or ivory, chopsticks were intended to protect people's fingers from heat, and were originally called *zhu*, or "help". They are now called *kuaizi*, a word that indicates the speed of the act, because chopsticks must move fast, and food should be presented in such a way that it can be eaten fast. The chopstick culture includes a precise strategy for cutting food before it is presented at the table, as with glazed Peking duck or Japanese sashimi. Bread does not exist in East Asia, for it is substituted with rice, which is cooked so as to release all the starches and facilitate the use of chopsticks. The various Japanese soba (buckwheat noodles), plain or served in broth, and Korean *kimchi* (vegetable preserves) are also meant to be eaten with chopsticks. The liquid is then sipped directly from the cup, and satisfaction is typically demonstrated by smacking your lips.

Even after exploring hands, breads, chopsticks, and serving styles, Asia remains a mysterious continent in terms of gastronomy. To scratch the surface a bit we need to concentrate on food products, especially the spices that have fascinated the Western world for centuries. In fact, a spice route across the Indian Ocean existed in Roman times, over a millennium before Marco Polo. The Roman *Apicius* is a collection of nearly 500 recipes in Latin, which call for liberal doses of pepper, ginger, cinnamon, and turmeric. Pliny the Elder lamented, "...in no year does India drain off less than 50 million sesterces from our empire, sending back goods which are sold at 100 times their cost price." The Latin word *species* was also used for these particular goods, which were subjected to the 25% customs duty on luxury items. Most of the spices came from India, and this collection contains recipes with cumin, hot pepper (included in various *masalas* such as curry), ginger, saffron, coriander, and pepper, without which South Asian cuisine would not exist. Other foods provide fascinating aromas (and sounds) as well: the phyllo dough, honey, and pistachios that make up baklava, attributed to Turkey here but also

found in Iran and Afghanistan in various forms; *bulghur*, a steamed and dried grain that is the basis for Lebanese *tabbouleh*, similar to Arabic *couscous* and Palestinian *maftoul*; Chinese *bok choy*; Indian *paneer* (cheese); Japanese *azuki* beans and tofu; Vietnamese *nuoc cham* (fermented fish sauce); the fragrant chives used in so many Thai dishes; and the pungent green *wasabi* that can transport connoisseurs with discerning palates from around the world all the way to the Land of the Rising Sun. And these are just a few examples of what Asia brings to the table. The list could continue to name a variety of cooking methods: Persian *pilaf*, where starch released by the rice is gelatinized; traditional Chinese bamboo steamers; and the Indian *tandoor*, an oven made of clay that cooks with radiant heat. All these techniques tend to concentrate and enhance the natural flavors of the food. Whether they were herders or warriors, the people of Asia ultimately granted the world an interesting and varied gastronomy that can only be truly grasped through travel; it's rare that restaurants serving ethnic foods, now so popular in the West, live up to the aforementioned traditions.

BAKLAVA

TURKEY

INGREDIENTS FOR 4 PEOPLE

2 3/4 CUPS (350 G) FLOUR

1/2 CUP + 1 TBSP (130 G) BUTTER

4 3/4 TBSP (100 G) HONEY

1/3 CUP (65 G) SUGAR

1.4 OZ (40 G) SHELLED ALMONDS, A LITTLE OVER 1/4
 CUP WHOLE

1.4 OZ (40 G) SHELLED PISTACHIOS, ABOUT 1/4 CUP
 WHOLE

1.4 OZ (40 G) WALNUTS, ABOUT 1/4 CUP CHOPPED

4 EGGS

3 TBSP EXTRA-VIRGIN OLIVE OIL

HALF A WHOLE LEMON

HALF A WHOLE ORANGE

1 TSP CINNAMON

SALT

It seems that this nut-based dessert (the name *baklava* derives from the Arabic word for "nut") dates back to the Assyrians, who apparently introduced it to the Greeks. The latter introduced the use of phyllo dough and spread it throughout the eastern Mediterranean, finding favor among Turks and Arabs.

Make the dough by mixing the flour, oil, eggs, a pinch of salt, and 2/3 cup of water. Let it rest for 1 hour. In the meantime, chop the almonds. Do the same for the pistachios and walnuts, but keep the three types of nuts separate. Mix together the sugar and cinnamon in a separate bowl. After 1 hour, turn the dough onto a floured surface and divide it in half. Roll both halves out until you have two extremely thin sheets. Cut 12 rectangles (6 from each sheet of dough) about 12 inches (30 cm) long, and lay 4 of them on a well-buttered baking sheet, slightly overlapping the edges. Melt the butter and spread a third of it on the dough. Then sprinkle it with the crushed almonds and a third of the cinnamon and sugar mixture. Lay another four rectangles of dough on top, just as you did with the first four. Brush it with the same amount of butter, then sprinkle it with the pistachios and another third of the cinnamon and sugar. Follow with a layer of walnuts and the remaining cinnamon and sugar. Cover it with the last 4 rectangles of dough, overlapping the edges as before. With a sharp, pointy knife cut it into 16 squares. Brush the top with the remaining butter and place the baking sheet at medium height in an oven that's been preheated to 425°F (220°C). Bake for 45 minutes.

Remove the baklava from the oven (you can brush the top with more melted butter) and let it cool. Meanwhile grate the rind of one quarter of an orange, then juice half of it. Do the same for the lemon. Pour the juices into a small pan, add the zests and honey, and stir on low heat. If the syrup is too dense, add 1 - 2 tablespoons of water. Pour it all over the baklava, then serve with a cup of Turkish coffee.

You can buy ready-made phyllo dough rather than making it at home. You can also use more than the 3 layers suggested in the recipe, but be prepared with enough melted butter to brush on all of them.

KEBAB

TURKEY

INGREDIENTS FOR 4 PEOPLE

Bread
4 CUPS (500 G) ALL-PURPOSE FLOUR
0.7 OZ (20 G) BREWER'S YEAST
1 TSP SALT
Kebab
2/3 LB (300 G) CHICKEN BREASTS, THINLY SLICED
2/3 LB (300 G) LAMB, THINLY SLICED

2 TOMATOES
2 CUCUMBERS
2 ONIONS
8 TBSP *HARISSA*
8 TBSP YOGURT SAUCE (OR *TAHINI*)
LETTUCE
PEPPER

Also called a *kebap*, it's one of the most popular Turkish dishes in the world. Though many different types exist, most stands and restaurants serve the variety known as *döner*, or "rotating". What rotates is a giant vertical spit with several layers of marinated meat slices, which are stacked one on top of the other to form a cylinder or cone. The *kebab* is sliced with a special device and can be wrapped in pita bread to make a sort of sandwich called *dürüm*, or served directly on a plate. Either way, the meat is always accompanied by sauces and vegetables. It's impossible to reproduce this exact process at home, but luckily the meat can be prepared in other ways.

Sift the flour and salt into a large bowl. Dissolve the brewer's yeast in 3/4 cup + 1 1/2 tablespoons (200 ml) of hot (not boiling) water. Add this to the flour and start mixing them together. Pour in another 1/4 cup + 1 1/2 tablespoons (100 ml) of lukewarm water and continue mixing until a consistent dough forms. Let it rise in a warm place until it doubles in size. Then divide it into 8 pieces and roll each one out into a disc (or oval) about 1/8 inch (4 mm) thick. Place them on an already heated baking sheet lined with parchment paper, and bake at 475°F (240°C) for 10 minutes. As soon as the bread comes out of the oven, put it in a paper bag. Then put a plastic bag over the paper bag and let it sit for 20 minutes to seal in the moisture.
Meanwhile, peel the onion and cucumber, and slice them very thinly. Slice the tomatoes as well and wash a few lettuce leaves. Heat a pan on the stove and cook the meat on both sides without adding any fat. Season with ground pepper.
Fill the bread with some meat, a couple of lettuce leaves, and a few slices of tomato, onion, and cucumber. Add a spoonful of *harissa* and yogurt sauce to taste, then serve.

Yogurt sauce lends itself to a variety of interpretations. There is a particularly popular version similar to tzatziki, *made with Greek yogurt and cucumbers. Alternatively, you can flavor the yogurt with salt, pepper, chives, and mint.*
Thinly sliced beef can be added to the chicken and lamb, and the meat can be grilled rather than sautéed. If grilling, the fire should be kept low so that direct heat doesn't make the meat too tough. All the meat can also be seasoned with cumin, mint, and other spices.

TABOULEH WITH VEGETABLES

LEBANON

Difficulty: Easy · Time: 40 minutes + resting time

INGREDIENTS FOR 4 PEOPLE

1 CUP (200 G) FINELY GROUND *BULGHUR*

10 MINT LEAVES

3 RIPE TOMATOES (OR 12 CHERRY TOMATOES)

2 PARSLEY SPRIGS

1 CUCUMBER

1 SPRING ONION

1 LEMON

1 BELL PEPPER, RED OR YELLOW

4 TBSP EXTRA-VIRGIN OLIVE OIL

SALT

GROUND BLACK PEPPER

If you want something fresh and healthy, *tabouleh* (or *tabbouleh*) is the perfect summer meal. This easy to prepare salad is popular throughout the Middle East. It's at its best in the Lebanese version, which also includes parsley (replaced with lettuce or other greens in some variations), and more than the indicated amount can be used.

Rinse the *bulghur* several times, strain it, and pour it into a pot with 2 cups (475 ml) of boiling salted water. Let it cook for about 30 minutes. Finely chop the spring onion and parsley, then peel and finely dice the cucumber. Dice the tomatoes and pepper as well, after removing the seeds and the tougher parts. Juice the lemon into a bowl, adding the oil and a pinch of salt. Stir well to combine.

When the *bulghur* is ready, strain it to remove any unabsorbed water. Mix the *bulghur* in a large bowl with the vegetables and mint leaves. Dress it with the oil and lemon mixture. Sprinkle with lots of ground black pepper and stir carefully. Let it sit for about 30 minutes before serving.

Bulghur *(also called* bulgur *or* burghul) *is sprouted wheat that's steamed and dried, then ground into very small pieces. The finely ground version is used for salads like* tabouleh, *while the coarser version is better for soups and stews. It has the same nutritional value as whole wheat. You can buy it in Middle Eastern grocery stores, or stores specializing in health food and organic products.*

GEFILTE FISH

ISRAEL

Difficulty: Medium - Time: 2 hours 45 minutes + cooling time

INGREDIENTS FOR 4 PEOPLE

1 CARP OR PIKE, WEIGHING ABOUT 3 LBS (1.3 KG)
1/2 CUP (125 ML) VERY COLD WATER
3 CARROTS
2 LARGE EGGS
2 ONIONS
1 TBSP FINE MATZO MEAL (OR BREADCRUMBS)

1 TBSP EXTRA-VIRGIN OLIVE OIL
1 TSP SUGAR
HALF A LEMON
HORSERADISH
SALT
GROUND PEPPER

A fish stuffed with fish - that's how *gefilte* fish is traditionally served. This Ashkenazi Jewish dish is eaten mainly on Saturdays and holidays. A large freshwater fish is deboned and the flesh is removed, leaving all the skin intact. A stuffing is made from the fish itself and then put back inside the skin, in a process requiring time and experience. For this reason, a "meatball" variation of the dish has become very popular. It tastes the same and is easier to prepare. The recipe follows.

Peel both the onions and the carrots. Clean and fillet the fish. Boil the fish head and bones in 6 cups (1.5 L) of water on medium heat. Add one onion and season with salt and pepper. Chop up the fish and combine it with the onion, oil, and one egg. Mix well and add the other egg (in some variations the second egg is boiled and mashed). Stir in the sugar, matzo meal, and cold water. Continue mixing and add a pinch of salt and pepper. If necessary, mash everything some more and add another pinch of matzo meal to thicken the mixture. Then form it into balls. Reduce the heat to the lowest setting for the broth. Drop the fish balls in, one by one, followed by the carrots. Cook for 2 full hours, and add some more water if too much liquid evaporates. Carefully remove the carrots and fish balls with a slotted spoon. Cut the carrots into rounds and place the fish balls in a deep serving dish. Strain the broth and pour it over them, garnish with the carrots, and let it all cool. Put it all in the refrigerator until the broth becomes gelatinous, then serve with a few slices of lemon and horseradish.

Matzah is an unleavened bread similar to a cracker. It's made with only flour and water, and cooks very fast. According to tradition, this is the bread the Hebrews made before fleeing Egypt, when there was no time to let the bread rise.

FALAFEL

SYRIA

INGREDIENTS FOR 4 PEOPLE

12 OZ (350 G) DRIED CHICKPEAS

2 GARLIC CLOVES

1 ONION, CHOPPED

1 TBSP PARSLEY

2 TSP GROUND CUMIN

1 TSP CORIANDER

1/2 TSP BAKING SODA

FLOUR

OLIVE OIL

GROUND BLACK PEPPER

SALT

Known as *falafel* (or *felafel*), these fried chickpea balls are very popular in Syria, Jordan, Israel, and all of the Middle East. *Falafel* is also found in Egypt, where it is usually made with fava beans.

Soak the chickpeas in water until they are well-softened, ideally for 24 hours. Once they're tender, rinse and drain them. Put them in a food processor with the onion, garlic, parsley, and coriander. Blend them well and transfer the mixture to a large bowl. Add the cumin, baking soda, and a pinch of salt and pepper. Stir it all together and let it rest in the refrigerator for at least 1 hour (tradition calls for the dough to be left untouched for half a day). Shape the dough into small balls, slightly larger than a walnut. Add a pinch of flour if the dough seems too wet. Put the dough balls back in the refrigerator, placing them in such a way that they will retain their form. After 1 hour, heat up a good amount of oil in a frying pan. When it's hot enough, fry the balls until they're golden. *Falafel* is eaten with flatbread, tahini (sesame paste), and a tomato and cucumber salad. You could also eat it with a bowl of Greek *tzatziki*.

Falafel can be eaten cold as well, but it's best enjoyed hot from the frying pan. Reheating after it's gotten cold is not recommended because much of the flavor is lost.

SABZI POLO

IRAN

INGREDIENTS FOR 4 PEOPLE
2 CUPS (450 ML) VEGETABLE BROTH
2 CUPS (400 G) BASMATI RICE
1/4 CUP + 2 TBSP (100 G) CLARIFIED BUTTER
1.75 OZ (50G) CHIVES
1.75 OZ (50 G) CILANTRO
1.75 OZ (50 G) DILL
1.75 OZ (50 G) PARSLEY
SALT

Sabzi polo is a rice and herb dish traditionally made for *norouz*, the Iranian New Year. *Sabz* means "green" and *polo* is equivalent to the Turkish *pilaf*, which refers to a method of cooking rice. This is the simplest recipe, though some variations may include scallions, fenugreek, garlic, and saffron.

Rinse the rice several times and leave it to soak in a large bowl for at least 1 hour, then strain it. Heat a large pot of salted water on the stove and add the rice when it starts to boil. Let it come back to a boil again and cook for a couple of minutes, then strain the rice. In the meantime, mix the herbs together.
Heat the butter in a pot, then spread a third of the rice across the bottom. Sprinkle half the herbs over it. Add another third of the rice and sprinkle with the rest of the herbs. Finish with a layer of rice and carefully even it out with a wooden spoon. Pour the broth over it, using the spoon to dig a few holes in the rice so the liquid will be better distributed. Cover the pot (so that air will not escape) and cook on high heat for 1 full minute. Lower the heat and continue to simmer for about 30 minutes, or until the broth is absorbed.
Turn off the heat and let it sit on the stove for 10 minutes. Stir it carefully, then transfer to a platter for serving. The layer of crunchy rice on the bottom of the pan should be served separately.

Sabzi polo is usually served with kutum (also known as "Caspian white fish"), a saltwater fish found in the Caspian Sea, where the average salinity is lower than other bodies of salt water. Though it belongs to the same family as carp, the flesh is more like sea bass.

BREAD WITH LAMB AND CHEESE

ARMENIA

INGREDIENTS FOR 4/6 PEOPLE

Bread

2 1/2 CUPS (300 G) FLOUR

1 1/4 CUPS (150 G) WHOLE WHEAT FLOUR

1/4 OZ (7 G) YEAST

1 TBSP EXTRA-VIRGIN OLIVE OIL

1 TSP SALT

Lamb

1LB (450 G) LAMB, CHOPPED

3.5 OZ (100 G) FETA CHEESE

4 GARLIC CLOVES

1 ONION

6 TBSP EXTRA-VIRGIN OLIVE OIL

2 TBSP *ZA'ATAR*

1 TBSP TOMATO SAUCE

2 TSP FRESHLY GROUND BLACK PEPPER

FRESH CILANTRO

MINT LEAVES

SALT

Some say it's similar to the Turkish *kebab*, but this lamb and cheese entrée is really an overview of Armenian cuisine. It's made from the country's most traditional food items: flatbread, lamb, and local sheep or goat cheese that can be substituted with Greek feta.

Dissolve the yeast in 3 tablespoons of hot water and let it sit for about 10 minutes. Mix the flours with the salt in a large bowl, then make a hole in the center and pour in the yeast. Stir everything together, slowly adding 1 1/2 cups (350 ml) of water. The dough should be consistent, not dry and not too sticky. Knead on a floured surface for about 10 minutes and shape the dough into a ball. Lightly oil the outside and place it in a bowl. Cover with a towel and let it rise for 2 hours. Knead the dough on a floured surface for a few minutes. Divide it into 4 - 6 balls of equal size. Cover them with a towel and let them rise for about 1 hour. Preheat the oven to 400°F (200°C). Roll out a ball of dough until you've got a circle (or a rectangle) between 1/4 - 1/8 inch (about 0.5 cm) thick. Lay it on a baking sheet, fold the edges, and prick the middle with a fork. Brush with water and bake for 20 minutes. Do the same for the remaining balls of dough.
Combine the meat, salt, *za'atar*, and 1 teaspoon of pepper in a large bowl. Mix well and let it sit out for at least 1 hour. Chop the onion and garlic separately, then heat 2 tablespoons of oil in a heavy-bottomed pan. Cook the lamb on medium heat, stirring until the meat is browned. Add the onion first, then the garlic a few minutes later. Wait another minute and add the tomato sauce. Stir it in well and turn off the heat.
Cut the feta into thin strips and finely chop a few leaves of mint and cilantro. Place some meat onto each base of baked bread, alternating with the cheese. Sprinkle with mint and cilantro and season with the remaining oil and pepper (or other preferred spices). Garnish each plate with a lemon wedge.

Za'atar is a mix of salt and herbs (thyme, sesame, and marjoram are the basics) that is very common throughout the Middle East.

NOODLE PAKORA

PAKISTAN

INGREDIENTS FOR 4 PEOPLE

3/4 CUP (100 G) RICE NOODLES

3.5 OZ (100 G) *PANEER* CHEESE

3/4 CUP (100 G) GRAHAM FLOUR

3 GREEN CHILIES

1 TBSP CHOPPED CILANTRO

1 TSP TOASTED CUMIN SEEDS

1 TSP SALT

1/2 TSP BAKING SODA

1/2 TSP GROUND HOT PEPPER

PEANUT OIL

Pakora is a popular appetizer in Pakistan, Bangladesh, India, and other South Asian countries. It's made with various types of vegetables (mostly spinach, onions, potatoes, cauliflower, and hot peppers) along with rice noodles and *paneer* cheese. Everything is coated in batter and fried in hot oil.

In a large mixing bowl, mix the graham flour with the baking soda, salt, cumin, and hot pepper. Add 2/3 cup (150 ml) of water and stir it carefully (you can use a mixer to save time) until the mixture is smooth and consistent, then set aside. Cut the *paneer* into cubes.
Heat some water in a pot and immerse the rice noodles. Let them cook for about 2 minutes. Drain them and lay them out on a cutting board or large plate to allow any remaining water to evaporate. Rice noodles can also be cooked without using the stove (let them sit in hot tap water for 10 minutes), but some brands do not lend themselves to this cooking method.
Combine the noodles with the *paneer* and the chopped chilies, then sprinkle with cilantro and stir it all together. Divide the mixture into small handfuls and heat a good amount of peanut oil in a large frying pan. Coat the handfuls of noodle mixture with the batter and fry them. Once they've browned, remove them with a slotted spoon and place them on paper towels to drain. Noodle *pakora* should be eaten while it's hot.

CHAPATI

PAKISTAN

INGREDIENTS FOR 4 PEOPLE

1 1/2 CUPS (170 G) ALL-PURPOSE FLOUR
1/2 CUP + 2 1/2 TBSP (80 G) WHOLE WHEAT FLOUR
1 TBSP CLARIFIED BUTTER
1/2 TSP SALT

It's the most common bread on Indian and Pakistani tables, but it can also be found in many other Asian and East African countries. It's round and flat because it contains no leavening, and it can be made with a mix of different flours (millet, barley, wheat, buckwheat, etc) or with wheat flours only. If no non-wheat flours are used, then whole wheat is the best choice.

Pour 3/4 cup (180 ml) of lukewarm water into a small bowl and stir in the salt. Measure the flour into a large bowl and slowly add the water, mixing well to incorporate. Transfer to a flat surface and knead for about 10 minutes, until the dough is firm and consistent. Let it rest for 20 minutes in a bowl covered with a towel.
Divide the dough into 8 little balls of equal size and roll them out into circles about 6 inches (15 cm) across. If the dough starts to stick, sprinkle some flour on the rolling pin. If you prefer smaller *chapatis*, divide the dough into more pieces. The size varies considerably among the different regions of India and Pakistan, and they can be as small as 2 inches (5 cm) in diameter. Heat a nonstick pan and cook the discs of dough one by one. The *chapatis* need to be cooked on both sides so flip them when bubbles start to form in the center, being careful not to break them. Remove each one from the pan a couple of minutes after it's been flipped.
As you remove each *chapati*, spread the top with a little bit of clarified butter and place it in a covered pan, laying one on top of the other. The pan should always stay covered to contain the heat and steam.

In Pakistan and India, chapati *is prepared with a* tawa, *a griddle pan made of metal or unglazed terracotta that distributes heat evenly over the surface of the bread. If you don't anything like this, you can use a nonstick pan as long as it has a very heavy bottom.* Chapati *can also be cooked directly over a fire by using a splatter guard as a sort of grill, though this does call for a certain level of experience.*

TANDOORI MURGH

INDIA

INGREDIENTS FOR 4 PEOPLE

Chicken
4 CHICKEN BREASTS (OR 4 CHICKEN THIGHS)
3/4 CUP + 1 TBSP (200 ML) PLAIN YOGURT
1 LIME
1 HEAPING TSP OF GROUND HOT RED PEPPER
1 HEAPING TSP OF CORIANDER
1 TSP GRATED GINGER
1/2 TSP CUMIN SEEDS
PARSLEY
SALT

Sauce
3 GARLIC CLOVES
1 ONION
1 SMALL PIECE OF FRESH GINGER
2 TBSP OIL
1 TBSP TOMATO PUREE
1 TSP HOT RED PEPPER, GROUND
1 TSP *GARAM MASALA*
1 TSP CORIANDER
1/2 TSP CUMIN SEEDS
1/2 TSP TURMERIC
1/2 TSP MUSTARD SEEDS

Tandoori murgh means "chicken cooked in a *tandoor*". This traditional Indian oven is made of terracotta and creates the effect of roasting and smoking at the same time. The *tandoor* is shaped like a cylinder or upside down bell and heated with wood or coal. It's impossible to perfectly reproduce this cooking method without a *tandoor*, though you can get very good results even from gas and electric ovens.

Squeeze the lime into a large bowl. Remove any skin from the chicken breasts and cut them into large pieces (if you're using thighs, remove the skin and then score both sides with a knife). Marinate the chicken in the lime juice for 15 minutes.
In the meantime grind together the cumin seeds, coriander, hot red pepper, and grated ginger. Transfer the mixture to another bowl, then add the yogurt and mix well. Add the marinated chicken and stir until it's well-coated. Cover the bowl and leave it to marinate in the refrigerator for at least 8 hours.
Take out the chicken and drain off the excess yogurt marinade, reserving it for later. Put the chicken in a pan and bake for 30 minutes at 425°F (220°C).
When you turn off the oven, pour the juices from the chicken into a bowl and put the pan of chicken back in the hot oven.
While the chicken is cooking, make the sauce by crushing together the garlic, onion, and fresh ginger. Use a mortar and pestle if you don't have a food processor. Grind together the hot red pepper, *garam masala*, turmeric, and coriander. Heat the oil in a pan, and before it starts to sizzle add the mustard and cumin seeds. When the seeds are toasted add the crushed garlic blend along with the spice mix you just made. Reduce the heat to the lowest setting and let it cook for 10 minutes, stirring occasionally. Add the reserved yogurt marinade and the bowl of chicken juices. Give it a splash of color with the tomato puree and then add the chicken, which should still be hot.
Let it cook for a few minutes. Season with a pinch of salt and a few parsley leaves and serve.

Garam masala *is a hot spice blend. There are many variations but generally, the main ingredients are coriander, black pepper, cumin seeds, turmeric, cloves, and cardamom. Hot red pepper, mustard seeds, garlic, and other flavors may also be added.*

KADAI PANEER

INDIA

INGREDIENTS FOR 4 PEOPLE

1 LB (450 G) *PANEER* CHEESE

0.22 LBS (100 G) BELL PEPPER,
    ABOUT 1 MEDIUM-SIZED PEPPER

4 GARLIC CLOVES

5 DRY RED CHILIES

4 TOMATOES

2 GREEN CHILIES

2 TBSP CHOPPED CILANTRO

3 TBSP CLARIFIED BUTTER

2 TSP CORIANDER SEEDS

2 TSP CHOPPED GINGER

2 BAY LEAVES

1 TSP DRIED FENUGREEK

SALT

Paneer is the most well-known Indian cheese. Popular throughout South Asia, it's a fundamental ingredient in many sweet and savory dishes. *Kadai paneer* is one of the most flavorful among the latter.

Grind the coriander and hot red peppers together. Crush the garlic, chop the tomatoes and green chilies, slice the bell pepper into long strips, and slice or cube the *paneer*. Heat the clarified butter in a pan and add the garlic. Shortly after, add the bay leaves, ground coriander and red peppers, and bell pepper. Keep the heat on low, and half a minute later add the ginger and green chilies. After another minute add the tomatoes and cook until the butter separates. Add the fenugreek (you can find it at health food stores) and season with salt to taste, then immediately add the *paneer* and cook for just a few minutes. The dish should be served hot and sprinkled with chopped cilantro.

You can also make paneer at home. For about 1lb (450 g) of cheese you'll need 1 gallon + 1 1/4 quarts (5 L) of whole milk and 5 tablespoons of lemon juice. Heat the milk, but don't let it reach a boil or form a skin. Then turn off the heat and add the lemon juice a little bit at a time. Let it sit for 10 minutes to coagulate. Pour it into a strainer lined with cheesecloth and rinse with cool running water. Squeeze the cheesecloth well to remove all the water and whey, then place the paneer under a weight and let it dry for about two hours. If you prefer a soft cheese that's ready to be eaten immediately rather than saved for other purposes, limit the drying time to 30 minutes.

LAMB CURRY

INDIA

INGREDIENTS FOR 4 PEOPLE

1 LB (500 G) LAMB	1 TBSP GROUND CORIANDER
1 CUP + 1 TBSP (250 ML) LIGHT BEEF BROTH	1 TSP CURRY POWDER (MEDIUM-HOT)
4 TBSP (60 G) CLARIFIED BUTTER	1/2 CUP DENSE COCONUT MILK
4 SLICES OF FRESH GINGER	1/2 TSP HOT RED PEPPER (GROUND)
2 GREEN CHILIES	1/2 TSP GROUND CUMIN
1 ONION	1/2 TSP GROUND BLACK PEPPER
1 GARLIC CLOVE	SALT

The mix of spices that westerners call "curry" is called *masala* in India. There are dozens of varieties, some hotter and some milder. In Tamil, "curry" means "sauce" or "soup", which are foods traditionally cooked with many spices.

Cut the lamb into 1-inch (3 cm) cubes. Clean and finely chop the chilies, chop the onion, and crush the garlic. Heat the clarified butter in a sauce pan and sauté the garlic and onion. When they've browned add the chilies, all the spices, and finally the lamb. Cook for about 5 minutes on medium heat. Add the broth, stir it in, and lower the heat just a bit. Simmer until the liquid is absorbed and the meat is thoroughly cooked (if the broth is being absorbed too quickly, add 1/3 cup of water and cover the sauce pan). When the meat is almost done, season with salt and add the coconut milk. Serve with plenty of basmati rice.

Lamb curry can also be made on skewers. If you prefer it this way, alternate the raw lamb with ginger slices, vegetables, and the occasional pearl onion. The prepared skewers can then be cooked in the same method as described above.

PORK VINDALOO

INDIA

INGREDIENTS FOR 4/6 PEOPLE

1 LB (450 G) PORK, CUBED

3 1/2 TBSP (50 G) CLARIFIED BUTTER

2 GARLIC CLOVES

1 ONION

1 TBSP PALM VINEGAR (OR RED WINE VINEGAR)

1/2 TSP *MASALA* (CURRY POWDER)

1/2 TSP GROUND GINGER

1/2 TSP GROUND HOT RED PEPPER

1/2 TSP GROUND CORIANDER

BLACK PEPPERCORNS

SALT

Vindaloo is a specialty of Goa, the smallest Indian state. Goa was long dominated by the Portuguese and the dish was actually "invented" by Portuguese colonists. They were trying to recreate the flavor of one of their own specialties, meat marinated in garlic and wine vinegar (the name seems to have evolved from the Portuguese words *vinho* and *alho*). Wine vinegar was not available in India at the time, so they used one made from palm trees instead. Indians then added other spices and adapted the dish to their own tastes.

Finely chop the garlic and onion together. Grind the spices and mix them with the vinegar in a small bowl.

Melt the clarified butter in a saucepan. Add the garlic and onion. As soon as they begin to brown, add the spice and vinegar mixture. Sauté on very low heat, stirring continuously. Add the pork with 3/4 cup + 1 1/2 tbsp (200 ml) of hot water, then cover and cook for 15 minutes. Uncover and continue to cook on low heat until the sauce has thickened. Add salt to taste just before you turn off the heat. Serve with sautéed vegetables and plenty of basmati rice.

In one version of the recipe the meat is marinated in the vinegar and spices before it's cooked, using 2 tablespoons of vinegar (instead of 1 tablespoon).
Like many Indian dishes, the amount of each spice can vary and others may be added.
For example, some recipes call for more garlic as well as the addition of cloves, cardamom, cinnamon, bay leaves, and turmeric. Depending on the spices used, the color of vindaloo *may also vary slightly once it's cooked.*

STEAMED DUMPLINGS

CHINA

INGREDIENTS FOR 4/6 PEOPLE

Pasta
2 CUPS (250 G) FLOUR
SALT

Filling
2/3 LB (300 G) GROUND PORK
1/4 LB (100 G) GROUND BEEF
1/4 LB (100 G) CHINESE CABBAGE, JUST UNDER 1/2
   CUP SHREDDED
1/3 OZ (10 G) FRESH GINGER

3 SAVOY CABBAGE LEAVES
1 SMALL ONION (OR 2 PEARL ONIONS)
1 LEEK
2 TBSP SOY SAUCE
2 TBSP SESAME OIL
2 TBSP SHERRY
GARLIC POWDER
SALT

They're called *zheng jiao* ("steamed dumpling") in Chinese, not to be confused with wontons, which use a lighter wrapper. The filling can be made with various types of meat and fish. One of the most common is a combination of pork and beef.

Make the dough by measuring the flour onto a pastry board and slowly adding 3/4 cup (150 ml) of water and a pinch of salt. Knead carefully for 15 minutes, until the dough is firm and consistent. Cover with a cloth and let it rest for 1 hour.
Wash the Chinese cabbage and clean the leek, then peel and roughly chop the onion. Grind them all together in a food processor. Grate the ginger and add it to the mixture along with the meat, soy sauce, oil, garlic powder, sherry, and a pinch of salt. Combine all ingredients well and add 1/2 tablespoon of water to moisten if necessary.
Roll the dough out to a thickness of about 1/4 inch (0.5 cm) and cut out squares of 2 - 2 1/2 inches (6 cm). If you prefer circles they should be at least 2 3/4 inches (7 cm) in diameter. Place a bit of filling in the center of each piece of dough. Close them carefully, bringing the edges together with numerous folds to create little "pouches" or half-moons. You can also lay another piece of dough on top and seal each dumpling like you would a pie, folding and pressing the edges.
In a pot suitable for steaming, line the steamer with Savoy cabbage leaves and carefully place the dumplings inside. Cook until the dough is almost transparent, which should take about 10 - 15 minutes. The exact time depends on the thickness of the dough and the level of heat.
Serve with a bowl of hot soy sauce (flavored with rice vinegar and a pinch of hot pepper) and a bowl of regular soy sauce on the side.

If you want to use a more traditional cooking method, line a bamboo steamer with Savoy cabbage leaves or lettuce. Carefully lay the dumplings inside and place the steamer over a wok of boiling water.

GLAZED PEKING DUCK

CHINA

Difficulty: Difficult · Time: 2 hours 30 minutes + hanging and resting time

INGREDIENTS FOR 4/6 PEOPLE

1 WHOLE DUCK, 3 - 4.5 LBS (1.5 - 2 KG)

3 TBSP WILDFLOWER HONEY OR 4 TBSP (100 G)
    MALT SYRUP

SALT

The recipe for glazed Peking Duck requires a great deal of time and skill. The preparation process is almost a rite; a codified sequence of movements. In the country that is home to the Great Wall, it really begins while the duck is still being raised. During the last two weeks the duck is actually fed four times a day on special foods that are very high in nutrients.

Ask your butcher to eviscerate the duck with a very small incision and cut the legs at the joints. If you find a butcher who can do so, ask them to make a small cut under the duck's trachea and blow into it, passing air between the skin and the flesh, and then massage it to distribute air over the entire body. This procedure makes it easier to remove the skin after cooking.

Rinse the duck's skin with boiling water 2 - 3 times, then hang it by the neck in a cool dry place for 4 - 8 hours. Dissolve the honey in a bit of boiling water and add a pinch of salt (some variations call for a bit of soy sauce, some use 3 tablespoons of vinegar, and some call for rice wine and sesame oil). Brush the mixture all over the duck, then hang it up again and leave it for a couple of hours. Set the oven to 425°F (220°C) and place the duck over a drip pan at medium height with the breast facing up. After 30 minutes reduce the temperature and let it cook for at least 1 more hour. Brush it with the glaze halfway through cooking (total cooking time will vary depending on the size of the duck). Some chefs suggest turning the duck and brushing it with glaze every 30 minutes, ending with the spine up.

When the duck is done, remove the skin with a sharp, pointy knife and cut it into rectangles, then remove the meat and slice it thinly. Arrange both the skin and meat on hot plates.

The duck meat and skin are usually brought to the table with very thin crêpes, *a plate of sliced spring onions, a cup of* hoisin *sauce (made with soy, garlic, sugar, and spices), and sometimes a shredded cucumber. You put a few slices of duck on a crêpe, add some sauce and vegetables, then fold in the ends and roll it up like a spring roll.*

OYSTER SAUCE
CHINA

INGREDIENTS FOR 4 PEOPLE
12 LARGE OYSTERS (OR 18 SMALL OYSTERS)
JUST UNDER 1/2 CUP (10 CL) HEAVY CREAM
2 TBSP (30 G) BUTTER
2 TBSP (15 G) FLOUR
SALT
GROUND CAYENNE PEPPER

Oyster sauce is an important ingredient in many recipes, not only in the Chinese tradition, but also in many other countries of Eastern and Southeastern Asia. It's available in ready-made bottles, but the quality of the homemade version from the traditional recipe is decidedly better. In fact, the preparation involves no artificial flavorings or monosodium glutamate - just real oysters.

Clean the oyster shells and open them up, making sure the liquid stays inside. If you don't have much experience, open them over a bowl to catch any spillage. Heat the liquid in a saucepan and when it's very hot, add the oysters. Leave it at low heat for 1 - 2 minutes depending on the size of the oysters (watch it carefully because the liquid should come close to a boil but should not actually boil). Shuck the oysters and chop them into small pieces.
Strain any additional the liquid from the oysters. Heat the butter in a pan and add the strained liquid. When it's about to boil, carefully add the flour, followed by the cream and salt. Simmer for 7 - 8 minutes, stirring continuously. Season with a pinch of pepper, add the oysters, and immediately turn off the heat. Let it rest for a few minutes, then transfer the sauce to a large preheated bowl and bring it to the table.

Oyster sauce is mainly served with meat and vegetable dishes. Among the most notable are green leafy vegetables with Chinese black mushrooms and sweet and sour beef (made with Savoy cabbage, ginger, sake, and sugar).

SPRING ROLLS

CHINA

INGREDIENTS FOR 4/6 PEOPLE

Dough
2 CUPS (250 G) FLOUR
1 EGG
1 TSP SALT
OIL
CORNSTARCH

Filling
1/2 LB (225 G) CHOPPED PORK
1/2 LB (225 G) SOYBEAN SPROUTS,
  ABOUT 3 1/2 CUPS

1/2 LB (225 G) CHARD, ABOUT 7 CUPS
  RAW
1/4 LB (115 G) MUSHROOMS,
  ABOUT 1 3/4 CUPS SLICED
3 *SINGADA* (WATER CHESTNUTS, CAN BE
  SUBSTITUTED WITH 2 SMALL CARROTS)
1 SHALLOT
1 CELERY STALK
HALF AN ONION
1/2 TBSP CORNSTARCH

1 TSP OYSTER SAUCE
1 TSP SOY SAUCE
OIL
SALT

Sauce
2 TBSP SAKE
1 TBSP BROWN SUGAR
1 TSP SOY SAUCE
CORNSTARCH

In China, spring rolls are eaten during the Spring Festival (Chinese New Year), which is how they got their name. There are infinite regional variations, including some sweet versions. This recipe is for one of the better-known savory versions.

Start the dough by sifting together the flour and a pinch of cornstarch in a large bowl. In another bowl, beat the egg with the salt and 1/4 cup (60 ml) of water. Stir it into the flour mixture, then add a drop of oil and another 1/4 cup of water. This should result in a sticky dough. Knead it, cover it with a towel, and let it rest for 1 hour.

Heat an oiled pan and add a ladleful of dough, cooking it into a sort of *crêpe*. Repeat this process until the dough is almost finished, saving 1 large spoonful for later. Grease the pan each time with an oiled towel or cloth and set aside the cooked circles of dough.

Make the sauce by mixing together the sake, sugar, soy sauce, a bit of cornstarch, and 1 tablespoon of water. Add 1 teaspoon of oyster sauce according to taste.

For the filling, cut the celery stalk into small sticks, chop the shallot and the onion (but keep them separate), and thinly slice the mushrooms and other vegetables. Separately, mix the meat with the cornstarch and let it sit for a few minutes. In the meantime, heat some oil in a wok and briefly sauté the celery and onion, then add the meat. In another pan, sauté the mushrooms with the soybean sprouts and the *singada*. Season with salt, add the chard, and cook for 10 minutes.

Combine the contents of the two pans and add the sauce, then the shallot. Stir well, cooking until the liquid is absorbed. Turn off the heat and let everything cool.

Now put a spoonful of filling in the center of each *crêpe*. Fold the ends inward and roll them up carefully. To better seal the rolls, you can use a bit of the dough that you set aside earlier. Fry them in a good amount of oil and serve them hot with sweet and sour sauce.

In one version of this recipe, the meat for the filling is marinated in a mixture of soy sauce, oyster sauce, and cornstarch. Marinating time should be about 20 minutes.

BIBIMBAP

KOREA

INGREDIENTS FOR 4 PEOPLE

2/3 LB (300 G) BEEF, GROUND OR IN CHUNKS

4 - 8 ASPARAGUS SPEARS

2/3 CUP RICE (A KOREAN VARIETY IS BEST)

2/3 CUP BEANS

4 EGGS

2 GARLIC CLOVES

1 ZUCCHINI

1 CARROT

1 HANDFUL OF SOYBEAN SPROUTS

1 TBSP SOY SAUCE

HOT PEPPER PASTE (*KOCHUJANG*)

TOASTED SESAME SEEDS

SESAME OIL

BLACK PEPPER

SALT

Bibimbap means "mixed rice". Eggs, meat, and especially vegetables (which vary according to season and individual tastes) are added to the rice. It's a very nutritious dish that's perfect for the colder months and even appeals to those who don't care for the hot and spicy flavors that characterize many other Korean specialties.

Rinse the rice and boil it in a small amount of lightly salted water. When it's cooked, strain the rice and set it aside.

In the meantime, boil the beans. Then tie together the asparagus spears and boil the bunch in salted water, making sure it stays in a vertical position. Keep only the most tender pieces when it's done.

Crush the garlic and julienne the zucchini and the carrot (or slice them into rounds). Heat the garlic in a pan with a good amount of sesame oil. Cook the zucchini in the same oil, followed by the carrot. Briefly cook the beans in there as well. Then add some more oil along with the soy sauce, and cook the beef. Season with salt and black pepper to taste.

Once it's cooked, arrange everything in heated bowls. First put some rice on the bottom of the bowl. Then lay separate piles of vegetables, soybean sprouts, and meat in a circle on top of the rice. Top each portion with an egg (or just the yolk), a tablespoon of oil, and a sprinkling of sesame seeds. Bibimbap should be served with hot pepper paste on the side.

In Korea bibimbap *is often served in a dolsot, a special stone bowl that can be found in some Western stores as well. There is a particular procedure to follow when using one. First rub the inside with a bit of sesame oil and uniformly distribute the rice over the bottom and up the sides. Then arrange some vegetables and meat over the rice and place the dolsot on the stove over medium-high heat for about 5 minutes. Just before turning off the heat, add the egg and let it set without stirring.*

KIMCHI
KOREA

INGREDIENTS FOR 4 PEOPLE

1 LB (450 G) CHINESE CABBAGE	1 TBSP DRIED SALTED SHRIMP (BEST IF THEY'RE
5 TBSP SALT	ALREADY GROUND)
3 SPRING ONIONS	1 TBSP SUGAR
3 GARLIC CLOVES	1 TBSP GROUND HOT RED PEPPER
1 CUP SOY SAUCE	1/2 TBSP GROUND GINGER
1 TURNIP	1 TSP TOASTED SESAME SEEDS
1 CUCUMBER	1/2 TSP GROUND BLACK PEPPER

Kimchi may be the specialty that best represents Korean cuisine. Prepared in a variety of ways, it can be eaten alone, as a side dish, or used as an ingredient in other recipes. One of its "ancestors" already existed 3000 years ago, when the practice of preserving vegetables in salt to make them available in winter became popular throughout Korea. Sauces, seafood, and other spices were added to the salt, facilitating fermentation of the vegetables and making them more flavorful until they evolved into the *kimchi* of today. Some families still prepare it in large earthenware jars that are buried and left to steep for months. The following is a quicker recipe, though it does require macerating time.

Wash the cabbage and detach all the leaves, throwing away the tougher ones. Put the good leaves in a large, shallow baking dish and sprinkle them uniformly with salt. Add a quarter of the soy sauce and let them sit for 1 - 6 hours, stirring occasionally.
Cut the cucumber in half lengthwise, remove the seeds, and slice it thinly. Slice the turnip as well, and combine the two vegetables in a bowl. Cover them with another quarter of the soy sauce. Leave them to macerate for 1 - 3 hours, mixing at least twice during that time.
Meanwhile mince the spring onions, garlic, and shrimp (if they aren't already ground).
Remove the turnip and cucumber from the bowl, drain off the soy sauce, and transfer them to a terracotta or glass jar. Strain the cabbage leaves and put them in the same jar. Add the garlic, sugar, sesame seeds, ground shrimp, ginger, spring onions, hot red pepper, a sprinkling of black pepper, and the remaining 1/2 cup of soy sauce. Mix them together and add enough water to cover everything. Cover the jar and leave it in a cool, dark place for a few days. The ideal would be to wait a couple of weeks.

Since the 18th century, the main ingredients in kimchi *have been Chinese cabbage and hot red pepper. Cabbage has always been considered a food with highly beneficial properties, while hot red pepper was once looked upon with distrust, perhaps because it was introduced by Japanese invaders. Many Koreans refused to eat it for a long time, suspecting that it was poisonous.*

Difficulty: Medium - Time: 30 minutes + macerating time

SUKIYAKI

JAPAN

INGREDIENTS FOR 4 PEOPLE

1 1/3 LBS (600 G) BEEF FILLET, THINLY SLICED

1 1/4 CUPS (200 G) COOKED RICE

7 OZ (200 G) SPINACH (OR HALF A CHINESE CABBAGE)

7 OZ (200 G) BAMBOO SHOOTS

3.5 OZ (100 G) *SHIRATAKI* NOODLES (OR CHINESE
   NOODLES)

3.5 OZ (100 G) TOFU

8 *SHIITAKE* MUSHROOMS

4 EGGS

2 CELERY STALKS

2 CARROTS

1 *NEGI* (OR 1 LEEK)

OIL

Sauce

1/3 CUP + 1 1/2 TBSP (100 ML) VEGETABLE BROTH
   (OR LIGHT BEEF BROTH)

6 TBSP SOY SAUCE

3 TBSP *MIRIN* (OR 2 TBSP SWEET SAKE)

1 TBSP SUGAR

Japan once adhered very strictly to the precepts of Buddhism. Cows could not be killed and beef consumption was extremely rare. Soldiers preparing for battle were the exception, and were allowed to eat *sukiyaki*. It was prepared outside, cooking the meat directly on the blade of a plow placed over the fire (*sukiyaki* means "grilled on the plow"). Today it's cooked on a portable stove right at the table.

Make the sauce by mixing the *mirin*, soy sauce, sugar, and broth in a large bowl. Boil the noodles, and while they cook, cut all the vegetables and tofu into relatively small pieces. Slice the mushrooms as well, but leave the caps whole.
Strain the noodles when they're cooked and arrange them on a large tray with the vegetables, mushrooms, tofu, and sliced beef.
Divide the cooked rice into 4 portions and break each egg into a small bowl.
Bring everything to the table, where there should be a portable stove. Turn it on, heat some oil in a deep pan, and add the vegetables. As soon as they begin to soften, add the mushrooms. Then add the tofu, and a few minutes later add half the sauce and the noodles. When the sauce begins to boil, reduce the heat and add the meat. As soon as it begins to brown, dip it in the egg and eat it together with the vegetables and rice. Occasionally top off the sauce in the pan.

The shiitake mushroom (in Japanese it literally means "oak mushroom") is the center of much sci-entific and medical research - apparently it has antitumor properties and reduces cholesterol. For some time it's been cultivated in Europe and America, where it's sold in many organic food stores.

TEMPURA

JAPAN

INGREDIENTS FOR 4 PEOPLE

1 2/3 CUPS (400 ML) SPARKLING WATER, VERY COLD

2 CUPS (250 G) FLOUR

8 SHRIMP (OR 12 SHRIMP TAILS)

8 ASPARAGUS SPEARS

4 SQUID

2 EGG YOLKS

1 EGGPLANT

1 ZUCCHINI

1 CUP SOY SAUCE

HALF A LEMON

SOYBEAN SPROUTS

OIL FOR FRYING

SALT

Today *tempura* is associated with Japanese cuisine, but its origins lay in European gastronomic traditions from the 16th and 17th centuries. In fact, it was Portuguese missionaries who taught the Japanese to batter-fry vegetables, crustaceans, and mollusks together. The dish was intended to make abstaining from meat easier for new believers (and for European sailors making stops in the Far East). The name tempura actually derives from the Latin *tempora*.

Shell and clean the shrimp, removing the heads, and straighten them as much as possible. Make a few small cuts on the underside, which will help to limit curling while they fry. Slice the squid, then wash the asparagus spears and dry them well. Slice the zucchini and eggplant into rounds (or relatively thin slices).

To make the batter, which should not be sticky, combine the egg yolks with the water and most of the flour in a large bowl. For best results, slowly pour in small amounts of flour, alternating with small amounts of ice-cold water. Mix well and don't worry too much about lumps.

Heat a large amount of oil in a wok. While it heats, lightly flour the shrimp and coat them in the batter, using tongs if necessary. Fry them a few at a time so the oil temperature doesn't drop too low (about 338 - 356°F/170 - 180°C).

When the batter gets crispy and begins to turn golden brown, place the shrimp on a plate lined with paper towels. Repeat the process for the squid, asparagus, zucchini, and eggplant.

Serve with salt, lemon (or lemon juice), a bowl of sprouts, and soy sauce. You can also put the sauce right on the sprouts to flavor them.

Other ingredients may be added or substituted when making tempura. *In the seafood category, prawns and oysters lend themselves particularly well to this frying technique. Among the best vegetables are parsley leaves, green beans, and peppers.*

SASHIMI

JAPAN

INGREDIENTS FOR 4 PEOPLE

3.5 OZ (100 G) TUNA FILLETS (AND/OR SWORDFISH)

2.5 OZ (70 G) SALMON FILLETS

2 OZ (50 G) TURBOT FILLETS (OR SEA BASS)

2 OZ (50 G) CUTTLEFISH (OR BOILED OCTOPUS)

2 OZ (50 G) FISH EGGS

1 DAIKON ROOT

HALF A LIME (OR LEMON)

SOY SAUCE

PARSLEY

WASABI (OR FRESHLY GRATED HORSERADISH)

GINGER

Many consider sashimi the height of Japanese cuisine. It consists of fish or shellfish, almost always raw, that is perfectly cleaned and finely filleted. The name means "pierced body" and likely refers to an ancient fishing method used in Japan. Once the fish was caught, it was immediately killed with a sharp spike and placed on ice, guaranteeing the highest quality product.

Clean the fish thoroughly, removing any bones or skin, and put it in a refrigerator set at a low temperature. Let it chill well, but make sure it doesn't start to freeze. Use a very fine, sharp knife to slice the turbot fillet into pieces about 1/4 - 1/8 inch (5 mm) thick, following the natural lines of the flesh. Slice the cuttlefish into thin strips about 1/8 inch (3mm) thick (you can then cut it again to get "sticks" of equal length).
Slice the tuna and salmon a bit thicker, about 1/4 - 1/2 inch (1 cm).
Arrange everything on a plate and add the fish eggs. Garnish with parsley, sliced lime, the *daikon* shredded into thin strands (alternatively you can slice a few radishes), and other vegetables if desired. The *sashimi* should be served with small bowls of soy sauce (or *ponzu* sauce), wasabi, and sliced ginger.

Sashimi *can be the main dish for lunch or dinner, but it's recommended as an appetizer (or should at least be served before other dishes) to keep any stronger foods from overwhelming its delicate flavors.*

AZUKI BEAN PASTE

JAPAN

INGREDIENTS FOR 4 PEOPLE

7 OZ (200 G) RED AZUKI BEANS
1 CUP (200 G) SUGAR
2 TBSP PINE NUTS
2 TBSP AGAR-AGAR POWDER
SALT

Azuki are legumes very similar to kidney beans, but they are smaller and have a fine white line down the side. They can be dark red, brown, or yellow. They have many beneficial properties, particularly when it comes to detoxification. In fact, they stimulate renal function, diuresis, and drainage.

To soften the *azuki*, soak them in cold water for at least 8 hours. Then boil them in clean water until tender. Strain them and save 1 cup of the water they were cooked in. Pass them through a sieve or food mill to purée.

Transfer the purée to a heavy-bottomed saucepan. Add a pinch of salt and the water you set aside. Cook on low heat, stirring continuously with a wooden spoon or whisk. When the purée is nice and hot, but before it reaches a boil, slowly pour in the agar-agar and the sugar. Keep stirring and reduce the mixture (this should take about 5 minutes from when it reaches a boil). If you prefer not to use sugar, you can substitute the same amount of rice malt.

Transfer it to silicone molds or small cups, let it cool, and put it in the refrigerator. If the paste doesn't thicken properly, bring it back to a boil and add another pinch of agar-agar.

Meanwhile, toast the pine nuts and grind almost all of them. Serve the cold paste topped with ground pine nuts, and garnish with the remaining whole nuts. As an alternative to pine nuts, you can use boiled and peeled chestnuts or sprinkle with cocoa powder. The dish is best paired with a cup of green tea.

In Japan, azuki *bean paste is also an ingredient in many more elaborate dessert recipes. For example, it can be used as a filling for sweet dumplings made with pastry dough.*

ZARU SOBA

JAPAN

INGREDIENTS FOR 4 PEOPLE

14 OZ (400 G) *SOBA* NOODLES
1 - 2 LEAVES OF *NORI* SEAWEED
1 CUP *DASHI*
1/2 CUP SOY SAUCE
1/4 CUP *MIRIN*
1 TSP SUGAR
WASABI
GINGER

Soba noodles are one of the most common ingredients in the fascinating Japanese gastronomic tradition. Made from buckwheat and shaped much like spaghetti or thin tagliatelle noodles, they can be prepared in many ways. *Zaru soba* is served dry and cold. It's accompanied by a very particular sauce, *tsuyu*, which is perfect for the summer months and a favorite among vegans.

Make the *tsuyu* sauce by combining the *dashi*, *mirin*, sugar, and soy sauce in a bowl. Make sure the soy sauce isn't too salty (if it is, dilute it with some water). Transfer the mixture to a small pot and bring it to a boil, stirring frequently. Then let it cool and place it in the refrigerator.
Heat a pot of unsalted water, and immerse the noodles when it reaches a boil. Leave the burner on and let the noodles cook for 5 - 6 minutes, then rinse them with cold running water. It's important to remove the starch so they don't become sticky when they've cooled. Let all the water drip off and arrange the soba noodles on a plate (or even better, on a bamboo platter as called for by tradition, which will allow them to dry perfectly).
Garnish with thin strips of *nori* and serve with *tsuyu* sauce right from the refrigerator, to which you can add some ginger and wasabi.
If you want to pair the *zaru soba* with another Japanese dish, hot tempura is one of the best. The temperatures and flavors complement and enhance each other extremely well.

Dashi is a particularly light fish broth made from kombu seaweed and dried, fermented tuna. It's used in many dishes from the Land of the Rising Sun and can be found ready-made in stores, in liquid or powder form. Mirin, on the other hand, is a rice liqueur that's similar to sake but sweeter and with a slightly lower alcohol content.

BANH XÈO

VIETNAM

INGREDIENTS FOR 4/6 PEOPLE

Batter

1 1/4 CUPS (300 ML) UNSWEETENED
   COCONUT MILK

1 CUP (150 G) RICE FLOUR

2 SHALLOTS

1/2 TSP SALT

1/2 TSP SUGAR

1/4 TSP TURMERIC

CURRY POWDER

OIL FOR FRYING

Filling

2/3 LB (300 G) BEAN SPROUTS (OR
   SOYBEAN SPROUTS)

1/2 LB (230 G) LEAN PORK

1/2 LB (230 G) SHRIMP, CLEANED

1/2 LB (230 G) FRESH MUSHROOMS

4 GARLIC CLOVES

2 TBSP OIL

2 SHALLOTS

1 TBSP FISH SAUCE

HALF A SMALL ONION

1/2 TSP SALT

1/2 TSP SUGAR

PEPPER

Seasonings and Condiments

2 CUPS (500 ML) NUOC CHAM

20 LETTUCE LEAVES

1.4 OZ (40 G) FRESH MINT, ABOUT 7
   TBSP

8 SPRIGS FRESH CILANTRO

1 CUCUMBER, PEELED AND THINLY
   SLICED

FRESH HOT RED PEPPER

The name means "sizzling cake". *Banh xèo* are rice flour pancakes filled with meat, shellfish, and vegetables. They're much larger in southern Vietnam than they are in central Vietnam (where they're called *banh khoai*). The recipe varies according to local tradition; recipes from northern Vietnam do not call for coconut milk. You can also make a vegetarian version with tofu instead of pork and shrimp.

These pancakes are popular in Cambodia as well, where they're known as *banh chiao*.

Crush the garlic and thinly slice the pork. Combine them with the salt, sugar, pepper, and fish sauce in a bowl. Mix well and let it rest for 15 minutes. In the meantime, slice the onion and the mushrooms, and cut the shallots into thin rounds.

Heat the oil on medium-high in a pan with an 8-inch (20 cm) diameter. Brown the onion, meat, and shrimp. Stir for a few minutes, then turn off the heat and set the pan aside.

In a bowl, mix 1 1/4 cups of cold water with the coconut milk, rice flour, turmeric, and half the shallot. Add a pinch of salt, sugar, and curry (not essential). Stir well to combine.

Heat 1 tablespoon of oil in a wok on medium heat, then pour in 1/2 cup of the batter in a circular motion. If you prefer an open pancake, distribute a small handful of sprouts over the surface. Add some shallots, mushrooms, 2 - 3 pieces of pork, and a couple of shrimp. If you prefer the traditional closed pancake, spread the filling on only half the batter and avoid the edges. Reduce the heat to the lowest setting and cover the pan, letting it cook for about 3 minutes (until the edges are brown and crispy). Then fold the pancake in half and slide it onto a platter. Keep it hot in the oven at 200°F (100°C) and repeat the process to make more pancakes.

If they're too big to serve, slice them into smaller portions and wrap them in the lettuce with a pinch of mint, fresh cilantro, and some cucumber slices. Put a bowl of *nuoc cham* (fish sauce flavored with sugar and lime juice) on the table for dipping the pancakes, and add fresh hot red pepper to taste.

GA KHO

VIETNAM

INGREDIENTS FOR 4 PEOPLE

2 LBS (900 G) CHICKEN THIGHS OR DRUMSTICKS

1/2 CUP (100 G) RAW CANE SUGAR

4 GARLIC CLOVES

4 TBSP OIL

3 TBSP *NUOC MAM*

2 SHALLOTS

2 SPRING ONIONS

2 TBSP GINGER (OR LEMONGRASS), FINELY MINCED

1 - 2 HOT PEPPERS (THAI OR JALAPEÑO)

1/3 CUP (80 ML) RICE VINEGAR

GROUND PEPPER

TOASTED WHITE SESAME SEEDS

SALT

HORAPA (THAI BASIL)

The various regions of Vietnam follow different recipes for *ga k*ho (caramelized chicken with ginger). Not only do the "secondary" seasonings vary, but also the ratio of meat to ginger. Regardless of variations, *nuoc mam* is essential. This fermented fish sauce is well-loved by the people of Vietnam, and similar to Thai *nam pla*. You can judge the quality by the color, which should be light brown or amber.

Debone the chicken and remove the skin. Cut it into small pieces and mix it with 2 tablespoons of oil, 1 tablespoon of sugar, and half the nuoc mam. Let it marinate it in the refrigerator for 30 minutes.

Meanwhile, mince the garlic and shallot. In a large bow,l combine them with the remaining sugar and nuoc mam, ginger, rice vinegar, and 1/3 cup of water. Slice the green part of the spring onions as well, into pieces about 1/3 inch (1 cm) thick. Finely chop the hot pepper. If you don't like things too spicy, you can substitute thin strips of bell pepper for the hot pepper.

Heat the other 2 tablespoons of oil in a pot. When it's hot, carefully place the chicken pieces inside. Leave the heat on high for about 1 minute without touching the chicken. Then add a third of the sauce you prepared and a pinch of salt. Lower the heat, wait another 2 minutes, and turn the chicken. Immediately after that, add the rest of the sauce and cook on low heat until it's thickened (the recommendation is to keep the pot covered for 10 minutes, though the complete cooking time will vary depending on the size of the chicken pieces). A few seconds before turning off the heat, add the hot pepper and the green part of the spring onions.

Season with pepper, sesame seeds, and a few leaves of Thai *horapa* basil. This dish is best served with a small plate of jasmine or basmati rice.

Thai basil (also called bai) *is an important ingredient in many Southeast Asian recipes and has a more fragrant taste than the basil used in Mediterranean cooking. Among the different varieties is* hora-pa, *used for soups and other hot dishes.*

LAHONG NHOAM SACH CHROUK PAKON

CAMBODIA

INGREDIENTS FOR 4 PEOPLE

1 MEDIUM-SIZED GREEN PAPAYA, OR TWO SMALL ONES (ABOUT 2.6 LBS/1200 G)

1/2 LB (230 G) SHRIMP, NOT TOO SMALL

1/2 LB (230 G) PORK BELLY, WITH SKIN

1 CUP MINT LEAVES, CHOPPED

HALF A SWEET ONION

SWEET FISH SAUCE

Lahong nhoam sach chrouk pakon means "green papaya salad with shrimp and pork". It's one of the most beloved dishes in Cambodia. It can be a snack to share with friends over good conversation, an appetizer, or the main course for lunch or dinner. If it's the latter, the salad is served with large amounts of rice. The combination of meat, shrimp, and papaya imparted by the Khmer tradition is particularly satisfying in the nutritional sense as well. In fact papain (from papaya) is an enzyme that promotes protein digestion.

Boil the pork in a saucepan with a small amount of water (about 3 cups). In the meantime, slice half a sweet onion and peel, clean, and chop the papaya. When the meat is cooked, remove it from the pot. Let it cool and slice it thinly. Boil the shrimp in the same water until they've taken on their characteristic pinkish-red color. Then strain them, rinse them under running water, and devein them. In a bowl, combine the meat, papaya, shrimp, mint, and onion. Dress the salad with fish sauce and serve.

In nature, papayas can grow as large as 20 pounds (9 kg), but stores usually sell the "babies" that weigh about 1.3 pounds (600 g). This happens because growers prefer the dwarf variety of the plant, since its cultivation is particularly lucrative.

TOM YAM KUNG

THAILAND

INGREDIENTS FOR 4 PEOPLE

4 1/4 CUPS (1 L) CHICKEN BROTH

7 OZ (200 G) BUTTON MUSHROOMS

8 SHRIMP (OR PRAWNS)

5 HOT PEPPERS

5 SLICES OF GALANGA ROOT (OR GINGER)

4 TBSP LIME JUICE

2 TBSP FISH SAUCE

2 CILANTRO STALKS

2 *KAFFIR* LIME LEAVES

1 - 2 LEMONGRASS STALKS

FRESH CILANTRO

Also called *tom yum goong*, this spicy and fragrant fish soup is popular in both Laos and Thailand. Shrimp or prawns are generally used, but they can be substituted with crab, squid, and many other types of fish. This is the Thai recipe; the Laotian version calls for a handful of rice added to the broth.

Heat the chicken broth and slice the mushrooms in half. Shell the shrimp, crush the hot peppers with a pestle, and tear up the *Kaffir* lime leaves and cilantro stalks (the latter should be washed well). Remove the outer sheath of the lemongrass stalk and chop it up.
When the broth reaches a boil, add the galanga, cilantro, lemongrass, and *kaffir* lime leaves. Cook for 15 minutes. Then add the shrimp, mushrooms, and hot peppers. Boil on low heat for at least 3 minutes and add the lime juice and fish sauce. Garnish with cilantro leaves before serving. Remember that the lemongrass, *kaffir* lime, and galanga are only for flavor - they should not be eaten.

Galanga is a plant that originated in China and is now well-known throughout Southeast Asia. It's known for its stimulant, digestive, and aphrodisiac properties. The name means "sweet ginger" in Chinese, and the similarities between the two plants make them interchangeable in the tom yam kung *recipe. The kaffir lime (also called Combava lime) is a citrus fruit similar to lime, but with some of the characteristics of citron. Its leaves are pungent and can grow to almost 5 inches (12 cm) long.*

MEE KROB

THAILAND

INGREDIENTS FOR 4 PEOPLE

2 CUPS (450 G) MARGARINE

1/4 LB (120 G) PORK

6 SHELLED SHRIMP

4 HANKS OF RICE NOODLES

4 EGGS

4 LEEKS (OR SPRING ONIONS)

4 GARLIC CLOVES

3 TBSP TOFU

2 TBSP SUGAR

1 TBSP SOY SAUCE

1 TBSP *NAM PLA* SAUCE

1 TBSP LEMON JUICE

VINEGAR

Mee krob is made from crispy rice noodles with shrimp and meat (or shellfish). Instead of pork, the same amount of chicken or crab is often used. The most common garnish is a mix of chopped cilantro and hot red pepper.

Heat a pot of salted water and cut the shrimp and pork into small pieces. Cut the tofu into small cubes, slice the leeks about 3/4 inch (2 cm) thick, and crush the garlic well. When the water is hot (it doesn't need to boil) immerse the noodles and let them cook for 3 minutes. Strain them and spread them on a cutting board or large plate so any remaining water will evaporate. Another way to cook rice noodles is to soak them for 10 minutes in a pot of hot tap water without putting them on the stove, though some brands don't lend themselves to this method.

Heat the margarine and fry a small handful of noodles, timing it carefully so you only turn them over once. When they've become golden brown and crispy, remove them from the pan and lay them on a platter lined with paper towels. Follow the same steps to fry the rest of the noodles. When they're done, break the fried noodles into pieces and pour a small amount of the used margarine into a separate pan. Lightly brown the garlic and leeks, then add ingredients in this order: shrimp, meat, tofu, some of the *nam pla* and soy sauce, lemon juice, and eggs (one or two at a time). When the eggs begin to set, add the noodles, mixing continuously. Cook for a few minutes, adding the rest of the sauces, the sugar, and a dash of vinegar. Serve the dish piping hot.

Nam pla *is a fermented fish sauce similar to Vietnamese* nuoc mam. *You can make it at home by crushing together the following ingredients in a mortar: 1 tablespoon of brown sugar, 1/4 cup + 2 teaspoons of sake, 1.75 oz (50g) of dried shrimp and/or small dried fish, and 2 gloves of garlic. When everything is combined well, add a bit of lime juice. Stir carefully and leave it to rest in the refrigerator for at least 5 days.*

NANAS GORENG

INDONESIA

INGREDIENTS FOR 4 PEOPLE

1 MEDIUM-LARGE PINEAPPLE
2 TBSP FLOUR
1/3 CUP SUGAR
1 EGG
1 TSP CINNAMON
OIL FOR FRYING
SALT

The words *nanas* and *goreng* crop up frequently in Indonesian recipes. The first means "pineapple", a fruit well-loved in this country, whether on its own or paired with other foods. The second means "fried" and refers to one of the most common Indonesian cooking methods.

Clean the pineapple, removing the stem, base, and skin. Cut it into 8 slices. If you prefer your fried pineapple to be ring-shaped, or if you don't care for the tougher parts, remove the core as well. Otherwise leave it intact - it adds flavor.
Leave the pineapple slices to drain. Combine the egg, flour, sugar, salt, and cinnamon in a bowl. Whisk it all together, and add a bit of cold water if the batter seems too dense. Dry the pineapple slices with paper towels and carefully dip them in the batter, coating both sides.
Fry them in boiling oil, flipping them over at least once, until they turn golden. Remove the pineapple from the pot, let the excess oil drip off, and serve.

Fried pineapple can be eaten plain as a snack, or sprinkled generously with sugar and cinnamon and served with whipped cream or vanilla ice cream.

NASI GORENG

INDONESIA

INGREDIENTS FOR 4 PEOPLE

1/2 LB (225 G) CHICKEN

3/4 CUP (150 G) BASMATI RICE

1/4 LBS (113 G) SHRIMP OR PRAWNS

3 GARLIC CLOVES

3 FRESH HOT PEPPERS

2 LEEKS

2 SHALLOTS

2 TOMATOES

2 EGGS

1 SMALL ONION

3 - 4 TBSP PEANUT OIL

1 TBSP SOY SAUCE

1 TSP *SAMBAL UDANG* SAUCE

SALT

GROUND PEPPER

Nasi goreng is a dish made with rice, shrimp, and meat (usually chicken). It's one of the few specialties that's common throughout Indonesia, a large archipelago nation where the cuisine differs a great deal based on region and ethnicity. Even so, this recipe has many local variations. The ratio of rice to other ingredients tends to vary the most, as do the vegetables.

Rinse the rice and boil it in a pot of water for 10 minutes. Strain it and put it in a bowl, breaking it up with a fork so the grains don't stick together. Let it sit for 2 hours (the traditional recipe calls for rice that was cooked the day before).
Mince the onion, garlic, and shallots. Remove the seeds from the hot peppers and mince them too. Combine them all with the *sambal udang* sauce and mix well. Dice the chicken or cut it into strips. Slice the leeks, and peel and dice the tomatoes.
Cook the vegetables in a wok with some peanut oil. When they start to brown, add the chicken. After 2 minutes, add the shrimp and tomatoes. Then cook for 10 minutes, adding the soy sauce and stirring frequently with a wooden spoon.
Meanwhile break the eggs into a bowl and beat them, adding salt to taste.
When the 10 minutes are up, make some space in the wok (or use a separate pan) and pour in the eggs. Let them cook as if you were making an omelet. When the "omelet" is ready, remove it from the wok and roll it up. Slice it into thin strips and return it to the wok, combining it with the other ingredients. Leave it on the heat for another 3 minutes, then add the cooked rice, leeks, and a bit of salt and pepper. Cook for about 3 minutes to let the leeks wilt, and serve.

Sambal *sauce is made with bell peppers and hot peppers. It's very spicy and there are numerous variations throughout Southeast Asia.* Sambal udang *is a version made with dried shrimp.*

OCEANIA

It's rather common to think of Australia as the land of kangaroos, a tourist cliché akin to a gondola ride through Venice. But it's a whole other experience to approach the subject from a gastronomic perspective. Australia is indeed the land of kangaroo steaks, and as much as that image might offend some sensitive souls, we must add that the flesh of this adorable marsupial has some excellent qualities. First of all, the tender, delicate red meat has a flavor that lends itself to the same cooking methods as beef. And then there are the health benefits: it's only 1% fat, compared to 16% for beef, and 3.5 oz (100 g) of meat has only 55 mg of cholesterol, which is even less than chicken. It also contains no traces of hormones, antibiotics, or other additives typically used in breeding, because kangaroos live in the wild. Most of the meat that's sold comes from Queensland and the Northern Territory, which are among the least polluted regions on the planet. Opposition from animal rights activists has recently weakened due to the opinion of many ecologists (even Greenpeace) that greater consumption of kangaroo meat in Australia could help lower greenhouse gas emissions considerably by reducing the presence of livestock breeders.

Our collective imaginations identify some other animals with Australia, and they too offer lean, healthy meats full of protein: alligators, which also come from Queensland, and ostriches (though technically they're native to Africa and were imported to Australia). Today they are easily prepared in many places, because these meats are imported to Europe and the United States, and ostrich can even be found fresh.

But these are not our only motives for a culinary voyage through the Southern Hemisphere. One of the most typical native products available here is actually the potato, though to be honest these potatoes are slightly unusual in terms of both their taste, which is sweet, and their shape, which is elongated with a pointy end. They're found in Australia, and above all in New Zealand, where they are called *kumara*. This traditional Maori ingredient was imported from the Pacific Islands and the three main varieties cultivated today, in increasing order of sweetness, are red, yellow, and orange. The best way to cook them is an ancient Maori method, the *hangi*, a rudimentary oven dug into the ground and "powered" by heated stones. Today the effects of this oven are recreated using various techniques, even in tourist hotels. But the food remains the

FROM SIMPLE TO CREATIVE

same: mainly potatoes, other vegetables, herbs, and meats.

Simplicity born of poverty seems to be the common gastronomic characteristic throughout Oceania. Brian Chatwin's *The Songlines* is one of the most enlightening books about aboriginal culture, and throughout the protagonist's long journey across the Australian Outback, we encounter only large steaks roasted over the fire and saloons battered by desert winds, where herders destroy themselves with whisky and gin. But hunter-gatherers still follow the diet of Australia's first inhabitants: they eat kangaroo, emu, wild goose, shellfish, Bogong moths, and sweet honeypot ants, not to mention an incredible variety of bush fruits, seeds, and berries, from *quandong* nuts to *akudjura* tomatoes and Kakadu plums. This recipe collection, perhaps unjustly, includes only two recipes from this longstanding tradition: grilled *kumara* potatoes, served with cuttlefish and Chinese *bok choy*, and a succulent kangaroo fillet. But it's hard to compile any official record of culinary conventions in such a wild, almost primordial world as the Outback. And it's impossible to research traditional recipes in a continent whose history (at least according to the parameters of the developed world) only began as a penal colony in the late 18th century, and whose residents immigrated from many diverse nations and brought along their own culinary traditions from their homelands.

Perhaps it's this lack of tradition that has given the new generation of Aussie chefs like Benjamin Christie and Vic Cherikoff the freedom to utilize local products and develop a modern Australian cuisine that is today among the most creative and sophisticated in the world; we might call this the Australian paradox. Even so, we did dig up a few historic recipes while flipping through "Grandma's recipe book". They were mostly desserts, like Lamingtons covered in chocolate and coconut, and Pavlova, a soft meringue with strawberries that was invented in the 1930s by a Perth baker to honor the famous Russian ballerina.

One final note about the Pacific Islands: Gauguin may not have been thinking about food when he left for Tahiti, but those sweet exotic flavors must have contributed to his poetic image of the "noble savage". We can sample them too, by making banana poe with coconut milk and fragrant vanilla, or grilling chicken breasts with pineapple and other tropical fruit. And, like Gauguin, we can convince ourselves that paradise truly exists.

KANGAROO FILLETS
AUSTRALIA

INGREDIENTS FOR 4 PEOPLE
1.1 LBS (500 G) KANGAROO, 4 FILLETS
4 TBSP WORCESTERSHIRE SAUCE
1 TBSP EXTRA-VIRGIN OLIVE OIL
1 TSP PEPPERCORNS
1/2 TSP THYME
1/2 TSP SUGAR
SALT

Kangaroo is a lean red meat, rich in proteins and minerals, and ideal for anyone following a low-cholesterol diet. It's not hard to cook, since just about any recipe that calls for beef can also be made with kangaroo.

To prepare the meat for cooking, rub it with a mixture of salt, pepper, and thyme (on both sides of the fillet). Mix the Worcestershire sauce with the sugar and drizzle half of it on the meat. Let it rest a few minutes and heat the oil in a nonstick pan. It's important to use a heavy-bottomed pan to evenly distribute the heat. When the oil is hot (but not yet sizzling), sear the fillets on high heat for 2 minutes, then turn them over and sear the other side. Lower the heat slightly and continue to cook. The total cooking time will vary based on doneness preferences. The recommendation is to turn off the heat when the center of the fillet is still pink. Remove the meat and lay it on a serving plate. Pour the rest of the Worcestershire sauce into the pan, stir, and drizzle it over the meat. Serve with fresh vegetables.

Kangaroo meat has a flavorful and delicate taste, so there's no need to go overboard on the seasoning. It also cooks well on the grill, seasoned with only salt, pepper, and a dash of balsamic vinegar.

STRAWBERRY CHOCOLATE PAVLOVA

AUSTRALIA

INGREDIENTS FOR 6 PEOPLE

6 EGG WHITES

2 CUPS (400 G) SUGAR

2 OZ (60 G) BITTERSWEET CHOCOLATE,
   FINELY CHOPPED

1.75 OZ (50 G) BITTERSWEET CHOCOLATE

3 TBSP UNSWEETENED COCOA

1 1/4 CUPS (300 ML) HEAVY CREAM

1 TSP CIDER VINEGAR (OR BALSAMIC VINEGAR)

1 TSP CORNSTARCH

1 PACKET (0.5 G) OF VANILLIN POWDER,
   OR 1 TSP VANILLA EXTRACT

STRAWBERRIES TO TASTE

Anna Pavlova was one of the greatest dancers of the 20th century. Ethereal, delicate, seductive, and romantic, she was loved throughout the world. In fact this dessert was dedicated to her. Though some say it was created for her 1926 tour of Australia, others maintain that a Perth baker invented it in 1935 - Pavlova had died young and he decided to honor her memory with a dessert that embodied the ballet star's attributes.

Start by preheating the oven to 300°F (150°C) and bringing the eggs to room temperature (if they're coming right from the refrigerator you can save some time by putting them in lukewarm water for a few minutes). Separate the egg whites and beat them until stiff. Slowly add 1 1/2 cups (300 g) of sugar, 1 tablespoon at a time. Continue beating until you have a firm meringue. Add the vinegar, cocoa, vanillin powder and grated chocolate, always mixing. If the consistency is not dense enough, add the cornstarch as well.
Line a pan with parchment paper and carefully pour the meringue in the center, forming a disc that's slightly concave in the middle. Place it in the oven and immediately lower the temperature to 200°F (100°C). Bake for about 2 hours. It should cool very slowly - the best way is to leave the meringue in the oven for a long time with the door partially open.
A little while before serving the meringue, slice the strawberries in half. Make the glaze by melting the bittersweet chocolate in a double boiler with the remaining sugar and just a little bit of water. Let it cool slightly while you whip the cream and transfer the meringue to a serving plate. Spread a layer of whipped cream on the meringue, top it with strawberries, and decorate with thin lines of glaze. Alternatively, you can sprinkle it with 3 tablespoons of bittersweet chocolate flakes.

The hardest part of making Pavlova is baking the meringue. More than baking, it really just needs to dry out. This is why relatively low temperatures are used and turning on the oven fan is recommended. If you're not in a hurry, reduce the temperature to 175°F (80°C) and leave the meringue in the oven even longer.

LAMINGTONS

AUSTRALIA

INGREDIENTS FOR 6/8 PEOPLE

1 LBS (450 G) BITTERSWEET CHOCOLATE

2/3 LB (300 G) SHAVED COCONUT

1 CUP (250 ML) COLD MILK

1 2/3 CUPS (200 G) FLOUR

2/3 CUP (130 G) SUGAR

7 TBSP (100 G) BUTTER

5 EGGS

1 (0.5 G) PACKET OF VANILLA POWDER

OR 1 TSP VANILLA EXTRACT

3 1/2 TSP (16 G) BAKING POWDER

Lamingtons are cubes of sponge cake covered in a chocolate ganache and liberally coated with coconut. This is the recipe for the basic version, which is the lightest, though they're often filled with cream or jam.

Beat together the eggs and sugar, then melt the butter in a double boiler. Add the hot melted butter to the eggs and mix well. Transfer the mixture to a large bowl and gradually add the flour, baking powder, and vanilla, making sure there are no lumps. When everything is well combined, pour it into a rectangular baking pan, about 8 x 11 inches (30 x 20 cm). It's important to butter the pan so the cake doesn't stick. Bake at 350°F (180°C) for about 30 minutes.

Make the ganache while it bakes. Melt the chocolate in a double boiler and heat the milk. Add the hot milk to the melted chocolate and mix them together. Be sure to keep the ganache warm. Take the cake out of the oven and let it cool for 30 minutes before removing it from the pan. Then transfer it to a work surface. When it's thoroughly cooled, cut it into 1 1/2 - 2 inch (4 - 5 cm) cubes. Use a large fork to coat each piece with the ganache.

Before it solidifies, roll the cubes one by one in the coconut flour, covering all sides. Shake them lightly to remove any excess coconut. Leave them to cool on a tray lined with parchment paper, then store them in the refrigerator.

It seems these sweets are named for Baroness Lamington, the wife of Charles Wallace Alexander Napier Cochrane Baillie, governor of the Australian state of Queensland from 1896 - 1901. With a passion for food and a big sweet tooth, she apparently encouraged her cooks to experiment until one of them finally presented her with a tray bearing the aromas of coconut, chocolate, and sponge cake.

LEG OF LAMB EN CROUTE

NEW ZEALAND

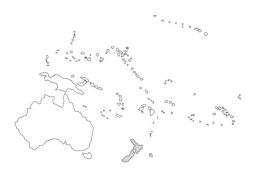

INGREDIENTS FOR 12 PEOPLE

1 BONELESS LEG OF LAMB

8 CUPS (1 KG) FLOUR

5 CUPS (120 CL) EXTRA-VIRGIN OLIVE OIL

1/4 CUP (25 G) YEAST

2 OR MORE GARLIC CLOVES

1 BUNCH OF PARSLEY

1 EGG YOLK

1 SPRING OF ROSEMARY

SAGE LEAVES

SALT

PEPPER

When it comes to New Zealand cuisine, lamb is king. There are about 40 million sheep in this country of farmers and breeders. At the root of this relatively simple delicacy, leg of lamb en croute, there lies over a century of careful breeding, the experience of generations of farmers, and a culinary technique that dates back to a time before British colonists arrived.

Chop and mix 2 garlic cloves, the rosemary, a few sage leaves, and some parsley. Add some salt and ground pepper, then rub the meat with this spice mix. Preheat a steam oven to 200°F (90°C). When the leg of lamb is thoroughly seasoned, fold it over and tie it with kitchen twine, then put it in the oven for 4 - 5 hours (time will vary based on the size of the meat).
Chop the remaining parsley and dissolve the yeast in a bowl with 2 cups + 2 tablespoons (500 ml) of warm water. Mix them both with the flour, adding the oil and a pinch of salt. Cover the dough with a towel and let it rise for 2 hours. Turn it onto a floured surface and roll it out to a thin sheet. When the leg of lamb is almost cooked, remove it from the oven, let it cool, and wrap it in the dough. You can wrap some garlic cloves or aromatic leaves in little pieces of dough, and place them on the outside to decorate.
Beat the egg yolk and brush it over the dough, then bake until it turns golden brown.

The steam oven is the modern equivalent of an ancient Maori cooking method. The original inhabitants of New Zealand actually cooked meat in what are known as hangi *ovens. These were pits dug in areas with naturally occurring steam. If no such geothermal effects could be found, the steam was created by placing heated rocks in the bottom of the pit and covering them with wet skins or other materials.*

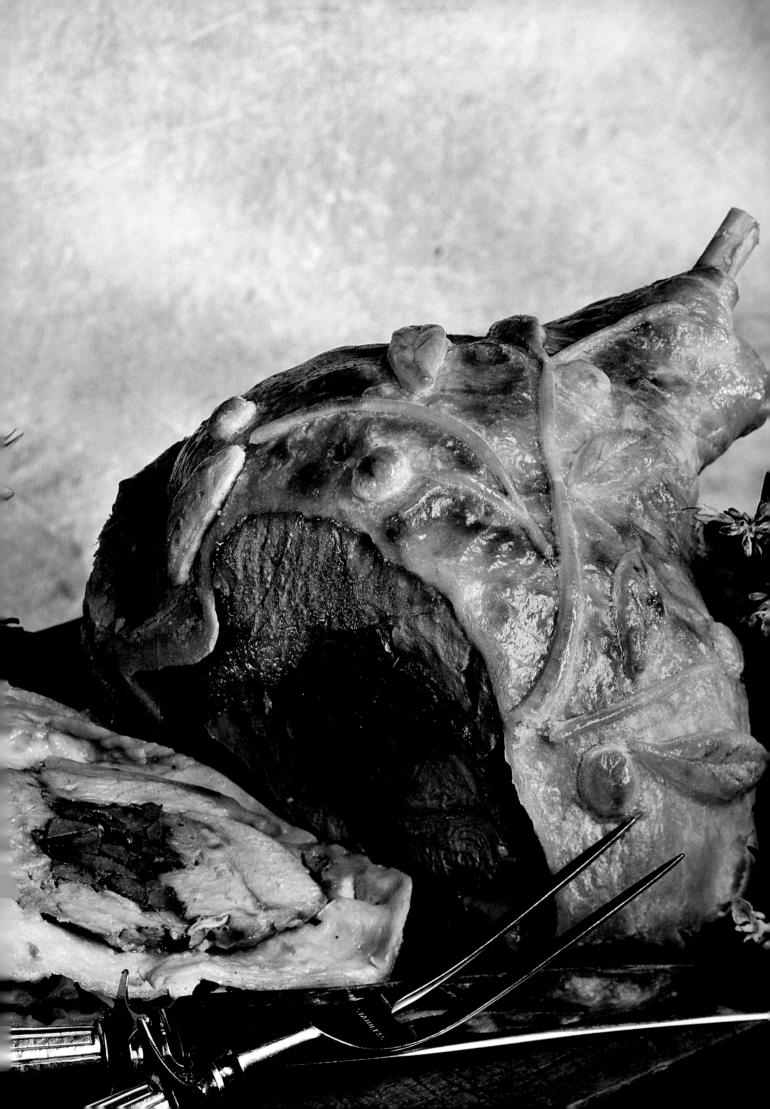

CUTTLEFISH WITH KUMARA AND BOK CHOY

NEW ZEALAND

Difficulty: Medium - Time: 50 minutes + cooling time

INGREDIENTS FOR 4 PEOPLE

Cuttlefish
4 CUTTLEFISH, ABOUT 1/2 LB (225 G) EACH
2 HEADS OF *BOK CHOY*
1 *KUMARA* (SWEET POTATO), 1 LBS (450 G)
EXTRA-VIRGIN OLIVE OIL

Kecap Manis *Sauce*
1 1/2 CUPS (350 ML) CHINESE DARK SOY SAUCE
1 1/4 CUPS (250 G) SUGAR
1 *MALABATHRUM* LEAF (INDIAN LAUREL)
1 SMALL PIECE OF *GALANGAL*
1/4 TSP STAR ANISE

This recipe is full of ingredients with unusual names that come from various places, demonstrating the wide variety of cultures that have influenced New Zealand cuisine. The sauce is made with *malabathrum*, a type of laurel with a scent much like cinnamon, which is common in India and the Himalayas. It's also made with *galangal* root (alternately known as *galanga* or Laos root), a type of ginger common in Thailand, Laos, and Indonesia. The official recipe cannot do without *bok choy* (Chinese cabbage) and sweet potatoes, which are called *kumara* in Polynesia (and Oceania in general).

Make the *kecap manis* sauce (sweet soy sauce) by caramelizing the sugar on low heat with 1/4 cup + 2 teaspoons (70 ml) of water, stirring frequently. When the sugar is melted, add the spices and soy sauce. Then let it simmer and thicken for 10 minutes, always stirring. Let it cool and pass it through a sieve.
Meanwhile slice the sweet potatoes about 1/2 inch (1.5 cm) thick. Divide the heads of *bok choy* in half. Clean the cuttlefish, removing the beak, bone, and ink sac. Separate the tentacles from the mantle and slice the latter lengthwise, into strips about 2 inches (5 cm) wide.
Make crosswise X-shaped incisions along the strips with the tip of a knife. Put them in a heated pan with the tentacles (heat should be medium-high). Turn them over and let the pieces curl up. After 2 minutes add 3/4 cup + 1 1/2 tablespoons (200 ml) of sauce. Turn down the heat, cover the pan, and cook for 15 minutes. Pour a bit of olive oil into another pan and cook the *bok choy* for 12 minutes.
Heat up a grill pan and cook the *kumara* slices on both sides, brushing them with some *kecap manis* halfway through cooking (the remaining sauce can be refrigerated in a sealed glass bottle). Serve the cuttlefish in their own drippings, with the *bok choy* and 1 - 2 slices of *kumara* per person.

WHITEBAIT OMELETS
NEW ZEALAND

INGREDIENTS FOR 4 PEOPLE

1/2 LB (230 G) NEW ZEALAND WHITEBAIT	1 LEMON
2 TBSP (30 G) BUTTER	SALAD GREENS
4 EGGS	SALT
2 TBSP MILK	PEPPER

"Whitebait" is usually a generic term for young fish (also called "fry") regardless of species. But in New Zealand, the word specifically refers to fish in the *galaxiid* family. They're river fish that are born in ocean waters because the current carries the eggs there before they hatch. As soon as they're born, they seek the river mouth and begin to swim back up.
New Zealand whitebait is also sold frozen, but it's not easy to find. You can substitute it with the same amount of young sardines, anchovies, or herring.

Beat the eggs and milk together in a bowl, and season with salt and pepper. Add the whitebait and mix well.
Heat the butter in a frying pan. As soon as it begins to sizzle, pour in the egg mixture and distribute it evenly over the pan. When the egg has set and the whitebait have turned white, flip the omelet and cook it for another minute. If you don't have a big enough pan for one large omelet, you can make four smaller ones.
Squeeze some lemon juice onto the omelet and serve it topped with salad greens. You can also add other raw or cooked vegetables according to taste.

In one variation of this recipe, the whitebait are mixed with the lettuce and served over the finished omelet instead of being used in the omelet itself. The omelet is very light in this case, and the fish needs to be boiled (but not so much that it starts to fall apart).

BANANA POE

TAHITI - FRENCH POLYNESIA

INGREDIENTS FOR 4 PEOPLE

5 LARGE BANANAS
2/3 CUP (160 ML) COCONUT MILK (OR HEAVY
   CREAM)
1/2 CUP BROWN SUGAR
HALF A VANILLA BEAN
3/4 CUP (100 G) MANIOC STARCH (TAPIOCA STARCH)

Many Polynesian desserts are made with bananas, or fruit in general, and the most popular is a Tahitian specialty called banana poe (or po'e). It's a sort of pudding that was once wrapped in greased banana leaves and baked in the fire pit, though today many Tahitians use packaged mixes from the supermarket.

Peel the bananas and cut them into chunks. Slice the vanilla bean open lengthwise and put it in a large saucepan with the bananas. Add enough water to cover everything, bring it to a boil, and cook for 15 minutes. In the meantime, preheat the oven to 300°F (150°C) and butter a pan. Remove the bananas from the pan and drain off any excess water (also set aside the vanilla bean) and blend them until a smooth purée forms. Transfer the purée to a large bowl and add the manioc starch (if you can't find it, cornstarch will work fine), some of the sugar, and the seeds from the vanilla bean. Mix thoroughly until creamy, then spread it in the buttered pan and bake for 30 minutes. When it's done, cut the banana poe into single portions. Sprinkle them with the remaining sugar and serve. To make the dish even tastier, pour a bit of cream or coconut milk over each portion.

Banana poe lends itself to many variations. One version calls for boiling the bananas with the skin still on. In this case they need to cook longer, and it's best to use fruit that hasn't been chemically treated in any way. Some other versions replace one or more bananas with other tropical fruits, like papaya, mango, or pineapple. If you do so the directions are the same, just make sure you end up with 4 cups of fruit purée. If the purée is too thin, you can add some more manioc starch or cornstarch.

HAWAIIAN CHICKEN
HAWAII - UNITED STATES

INGREDIENTS FOR 4 PEOPLE

1 LB (450 G) CHICKEN BREAST, ALREADY CLEANED

10 OZ (270 G) FRESH PINEAPPLE, JUST UNDER 2
   CUPS CUT INTO CHUNKS

8.8 OZ (250 G) RED BELL PEPPER, ABOUT 2
   MEDIUM PEPPERS

OIL

SALT

PEPPER

Hawaiian cooking, much like Polynesian cooking, is not afraid to mix flavors. Meat, tropical fruit, and vegetables are often used together for recipes rich in flavor and fantasy. Hawaiian chicken is one of the most well-known and emblematic dishes, both easy to prepare and a surprise for the Western palate.

Remove the seeds and membrane from the pepper, and cut it lengthwise into thin slices. Dice the chicken and the pineapple. Sauté the pineapple with a bit of oil and season with salt and pepper to taste. Then remove the pineapple and cook the chicken in the same pan, adding another dash of oil. Add the pepper shortly after the chicken.
When the chicken is almost done, add the cooked pineapple. Turn up the heat and cook everything together for 3 minutes.
Hawaiian chicken can be served with rice that's been cooked in vegetable broth and seasoned with curry.

This dish can be made in many different ways. One variety calls for other diced tropical fruits to be cooked with the pineapple. Another calls for 10 ounces of pearl onions to be boiled, cooked with sugar and vinegar, and added to the pineapple, meat, and peppers.

SESAME CRUSTED MAHI MAHI

HAWAII - UNITED STATES

INGREDIENTS FOR 4 PEOPLE

4 MAHI-MAHI FILLETS
4 TBSP WHITE SESAME SEEDS
2 TBSP SESAME OIL
1 TBSP EXTRA-VIRGIN OLIVE OIL

Mahi-mahi is a fish that can grow up to 6 1/2 feet (2 m) long and weight up to 44 pounds (20 kg). Also known as dolphin-fish or dorado, it's not limited to exotic tropical waters - it's found in the Mediterranean too. They're more easily caught in the fall, when they move toward the coasts to lay their eggs. If you can't find it at the fish market you can substitute greater amberjack.

Rinse the fillets and gently pat them dry with paper towels. If they're very thick, slice them into equally-sized pieces. Rub sesame oil on both sides of each fillet. Sprinkle sesame seeds only on the skinless side.
Pour a bit of extra-virgin olive oil into a wok or nonstick pan over medium heat. When it's hot, lay the fillets in the pan with the sesame side down. Cook for 4 minutes, then carefully turn the fillets over and cook for another 3 - 5 minutes (time will vary depending on the thickness of the slices).

Sesame crusted mahi-mahi fillets are generally served on a bed of vegetables, and finely sliced peppers are a must. They're a common ingredient in Hawaiian cooking and their bright colors are almost symbolic of its light and healthy nature.

AMERICA

The day a Spanish sailor saw land from the crow's nest of the *Pinta* marked a worldwide revolution in food and agriculture: October 12, 1492. His shout put an end to the Middle Ages and signaled victory for Christopher Columbus. But, the victory was hollow because the explorer had not arrived in the Indies, where he'd hoped collect spices, silk, and precious stones. Instead, he had found a small island in the Bahamas that offered everything but the treasures so coveted by European courts. Subsequent voyages by Columbus and his colleagues never bore the desired fruit, and though Hernán Cortés had looted an enormous amount of Aztec gold from Mexico, he still regretted that he hadn't found cloves and nutmeg. By the 17th century, it was clear to Europeans that the Americas were not a spice paradise. But in the meantime, several products had crossed the Atlantic that would forever change the diets of Europe and some even of Asia. Among them were tomatoes, pumpkins, cocoa, pineapple, and many varieties of beans. But the two plants destined to become most irreplaceable parts of everyday European in everyday life were corn, which yielded ten times the harvest of other grains and required less irrigation, and the nutritious potato, which was an excellent alternative to bread. It's also not entirely true that no spices came from the Americas. As Columbus wrote: "There is also plenty of *ají*, which is their pepper, which is more valuable than [black] pepper, and all the people eat nothing else, it being very wholesome." This refers to *Capsicum chinense*, specifically the *habanero* variety. It was called *asci* in Antillean (the origin of the Spanish *ají*), *chili* in Nahuatl, and *pepe* or *peperoncino* (from the Latin *piper*) in Italian, for its similarity in flavor to black peppercorns. The chili pepper, which had been cultivated in Mexico since the end of the 6th millennium BC, enjoyed worldwide success after Columbus's discovery and became the most commonly used seasoning in Asian and African cuisine as well.

But the flow of products was not one-way. The Americas also imported plants, and especially animals from Europe, which were unknown to the native populations of both North and South America: sugarcane, horses, and rice. The Antilles became the biggest producer of sugarcane in the world, we wouldn't even have the Western cinema genre without the horse (it's impossible to imagine Tashunca Witco, also known as Crazy Horse, without his Appaloosa), and rice cultivation was first attempted in Virginia in 1647. In fact, it was rice, originally from China, which made

COOKING IN THE NEW WORLD

the long journey to the West and invaded all culinary traditions in the New World. Until this point, the Americas had only used a similar wild grain (known as Northern wild rice, which is really a variety of zizania). The pig also made this long journey, from domestication in China around 5000 BC all the way to the modern American hot dog. Even cattle, destined to make the ubiquitous American hamburger, whose fate lay with McDonald's and similar chains, are of Eurasian and African origin.

It is essential to consider the migration of foodstuffs from East to West and vice versa when we talk about American gastronomy. And if we exclude any remnants of native cuisine from Central and South America, and the resulting culture of corn, cassava, and plantains (like firmer, greener bananas, they're only eaten cooked and are a staple of these culinary traditions), what's left is European, echoing the culinary conventions of the colonists' home countries: England, France, Spain, and Portugal. Here we have some cases of "hybridization" among various food products and traditions.

One of the most successful pairings in Central American cooking is rice (Asian origin) and black beans (native origin). In its basic form it's called *gallo pinto*, in reference to the black and white plumage of a *gallo* (rooster). It is the national dish of Costa Rica and Nicaragua, but also very popular under other names in Cuba (*moros y cristianos*), Perù (*tacu tacu*), and Colombia (*calentado paisa*). We present a Venezuelan recipe in this collection, *pabellón crollo* (also a national dish), which adds beef and plantains to the rice and beans. This combination is also a typical side dish for Haitian *griot*, where the most prominent ingredient is fried pork (along with plantains of course).

Beans lend their name to the best-known Brazilian recipe, *fejoada*, which bounced from Portugal to South America and is a perfect example of gastronomic mixing. Various cuts of pork are combined with black beans (Cariocan version) or brown beans (in Bahía), and everything is served with rice, chili pepper, and *farofa* (cassava flour) in an extraordinary blend of flavors and origins.

Beans are found in Mexico as well, where they join rice, corn, chili peppers, and various meats to fill tacos and burritos or make chili con carne, the tastiest example of Tex-Mex.

Continuing our search for hybridization in Mexico, we come across guacamole. The recipe for this well-known avocado dip is native to the area, though it now includes lots of ground pepper (unknown to the Aztecs). And don't forget that many of these dishes, especially chili and guacamole, are always served with corn tortillas, which have become a modern appetizer in the form of nachos (apparently triangular corn chips were not invented until 1943).

Corn is called *jojoto* in Venezuela and it's used to make cakes, soufflés, and puddings. This grain originated in the Mexican region of Oaxaca and has also been around in Andean countries for a very long time. It's the first of two elements that form the culinary foundation of South America. The other element, beef, is entirely from Europe. Just like the Argentinian Pampas, the Brazilian Pantanal turned out to be an ideal space for raising cattle. And the *gauchos* out on those grassy plains with their *bolas*, traditional garb, nomadic life, and a cooking style that naturally utilized basic techniques suited to the outdoors, have been the stuff of legends since the 18th century. This collection includes *asado* and *churrasco*, more interesting for the lifestyle they evoke than for their flavors (which depend on the quality of the meat).

The recipe for *empanadas* also goes with the cowboy lifestyle. These fried dumplings filled with beef and served with *asado* were made to celebrate the gauchos' return from the pastures. *Empanadas* are actually a transversal food, found from Patagonia to Colombia. In the latter, we find the *antioqueñas* version, which uses cornmeal in the coating and livens up the beef filling with chili pepper.

We can also find culinary hybrids up in North America, though at first glance the gastronomic culture appears to be derived entirely from Europe. Let's take the example of pancakes, the most common breakfast element in Canada and the U.S. They probably started in Great Britain, even if the French crêpe was the original model. But they're improved with an entirely American product: syrup extracted from maple trees, which the native Iroquois also knew how to produce. The pancake recipe here is attributed to Canada in honor of the national symbol (a maple leaf) on the flag.

One of the most famous American meals is the traditional, roasted Thanksgiving turkey. The story dates back to the first colonies and the difficulties faced by colonists in adapting their cooking. We're talking about the Pilgrims, who left England aboard the Mayflower and reached Massachusetts in 1621. They were decimated by the terrible winter when the seeds they brought from their homeland couldn't produce enough food. The following year the Native Americans taught them to harvest berries, cultivate corn, and cook turkey (long domesticated in Europe, wild turkey is still common in American forests between Ohio and Tennessee). As in the tale of Pocahontas, the Pilgrims gave a dinner of Thanksgiving to show their gratitude, the same dinner that's been celebrated every fourth Thursday in November for nearly four centuries. While legend holds that the Pilgrims offered a dinner of Thanksgiving to show gratitude to their Native American friends, such a dinner very likely never occurred. The reality is that notion of an annual Thanksgiving dinner was invented after the Civil War, in an effort to forge national unity after the terrible and divisive war years. Still, the tradition holds, and on the fourth Thursday of November, Americans feast at their dinner tables and give thanks for family, friends, health and prosperity.

Peanuts are another food that was given introduced to the colonists by the native populations. The plant originated in South America and produces decidedly caloric seeds. In Europe they're usually eaten toasted, or crushed to extract their wonderful oil (they contain up to 50 percent), but in the United States they're more commonly consumed in the form of peanut butter, which comes in both natural and sugar-laden forms. (Categorized as junk food, it has contributed to obesity.) But here, we've chosen to highlight a curious local recipe: Williamsburg cream of peanut soup, a classic Virginian dish.

And finally, we conclude with something sweet, a dessert that may be most identified with the United States, particularly New York, but in fact has such a long and ancient history and is so popular throughout the world that it's the best example of hybridization out there: cheesecake. References to desserts made with cheese, honey, and spices such as laurel can be found in Ancient Greece (it's mentioned by Callimachus) and Rome (Cato the Censor). Recipes come from all over the planet, from Sicily to Japan. However, true cheesecake was a child of the first food industry, when an Ontario milkman (he later immigrated to Chicago) named James L. Kraft created a spreadable cheese by accident in 1903, and called it "Philadelphia". His invention marked the birth of an empire that was destined to evolve into the largest multinational business in the world and become the basis for a truly decadent recipe, a history that strikes us as quintessentially American.

PANCAKES

CANADA

INGREDIENTS FOR 4 PEOPLE

2 CUPS (475 ML) MILK
2 1/4 CUPS (280 G) FLOUR
1/4 CUP (60 G) BUTTER
3 EGGS
1 TBSP BROWN SUGAR
1 TSP BAKING SODA
1 TSP SALT

It's not a true Canadian breakfast without pancakes, those crêpes made from flour, milk, and butter that are cooked in a frying pan and rise over a 1/2 inch (1 cm) high. There are many variations despite the simplicity of the recipe. For example, the batter includes a bit of yogurt in some areas, while others substitute oil for the butter.

Sift the flour into a bowl and add the sugar, salt, and baking soda. Mix thoroughly and create a well. Separate the eggs. Briefly beat the yolks and whip the whites into stiff peaks. Melt the butter in a small pot and stir in the milk.
Add the egg yolks to the bowl and start mixing. Add the milk and butter, then the egg whites. Continue mixing until well combined.
Grease a small nonstick frying pan (about 4 inches/10 cm) and heat it on the stove. Pour in 3 heaping tablespoons of the batter and distribute it evenly over the bottom of the pan. Cook on low heat for 2 - 3 minutes, or at least until the side that's facing up sets, turning bubbly and porous. Flip the pancake with a spatula and continue to cook until it's golden brown.
Repeat the process until all the batter is gone, greasing the pan between pancakes. Serve them hot with lots of maple syrup (or very liquid honey), jam, and peanut butter.

Maple syrup is the most traditional Canadian sweetener. It's made by boiling the sap from black maple and sugar maple trees, which are mainly found in Québec. The sap is extracted between March and April, when winter is over but the trees are still in a dormant state.

TOURTIÈRE DU RÉVEILLON

CANADA

INGREDIENTS FOR 6/8 PEOPLE

2 LBS (900 G) GROUND PORK

5 1/2 CUPS (660 G) FLOUR

1 1/2 CUPS + 4 TSP (375 ML) BEEF BROTH

1 CUP (225 G) BUTTER

1 CUP (150 G) BUTTON MUSHROOMS

1/3 CUP + 1 1/2 TBSP (100 ML) VERY COLD WATER

3 SMALL ONIONS

3 GARLIC CLOVES

1 EGG

1 CELERY STALK

1 BUNCH OF PARSLEY

3 TBSP BREADCRUMBS

1 TBSP OIL

1/2 TSP PEPPER

1/2 TSP SAVORY

1/2 TSP CINNAMON

CLOVES

SALT

In French-speaking Canada, especially Québec, *tourtière du réveillon* ("revelry meat pie") is the traditional Christmas and New Year's party specialty. Each family has its own recipe handed down over many generations. The key ingredient is ground pork, while the amounts and types of spices and vegetables can vary.

Cut the butter into small pieces and put it back in the refrigerator. Put the flour in a food processor with 1 teaspoon of salt. Add the cold butter and pulse, gradually adding the cold water as well. If the dough is too dry, add another 4 teaspoons (20 ml) of water. Turn it onto a flat surface and work the dough a bit (don't worry if there are still visible bits of butter). Let it rest for a few minutes, then divide it in half and form 2 balls. Roll them both out into equal-sized discs, about 8 1/2 - 10 inches (22 - 25 cm) across. Refrigerate them for at least 1 hour.
Heat the broth and clean and slice the mushrooms. Peel the onion and garlic, and mince them. Chop up the parsley and celery as well. Heat the oil in a large pot on high heat and brown the meat for 10 minutes. If a lot of liquid is produced, remove it from the pot with a spoon. When 10 minutes are up, add the garlic, onion, mushrooms, celery, savory, pepper, cinnamon, 2 cloves, and salt to taste. Let all the flavors cook together for a minute, then add the broth. Cover the pot and reduce the heat as soon as it starts to simmer. Cook for about 40 minutes, then add the breadcrumbs and parsley. If there's too much liquid left, add more breadcrumbs. Let it cool.
Preheat the oven to 375°F (190°C) and lay one disc of dough on the bottom of a pie pan. Pour in the meat mixture and spread it evenly over the crust. Cover the pie with the second disc of dough and seal the edges.
Beat the egg and brush it over the top of the pie. Make a small cut to let the steam escape (or remove a small piece of dough) and bake for about 45 minutes.

PASTRAMI

UNITED STATES

INGREDIENTS FOR 16 PEOPLE

1 BEEF BRISKET, ABOUT 7 1/2 LBS (3.5 KG)

4.2 OZ (120 G) COARSE SALT

1/4 CUP + 1 TSP (60 G) BROWN SUGAR, PACKED

5 TBSP (30 G) CORIANDER SEEDS

4 TBSP + 2 TSP (30 G) COARSELY GROUND BLACK
   PEPPER

1 OZ (30 G) FRESHLY GRATED GINGER

2 1/2 TBSP (15 G) COARSELY GROUND ALLSPICE

1 HEAD OF GARLIC

1/4 TSP SALTPETER

HERBS

Pastrami is smoked and brined meat that was brought to America by Jewish immigrants from Romania and Moldavia. Today you can buy it ready-made, for sandwiches and more complicated recipes. You can also make it at home, but it takes experience, patience, and a meat smoker.

Grind the coriander and crush more than half the garlic. Mix them with the ginger and half the pepper and allspice. Put a pot with 3 quarts (3 L) of water on the stove, and add the salt and sugar. When it's hot, add the herbs and spices. Then turn off the heat, add the saltpeter, and let it cool. Remove the excess fat from the meat. Put the meat in a bowl and pour the water and spice mix over it. Then transfer it all to a sealable plastic bag. Get all the air out and close the bag. Put it in the refrigerator for 12 days. Turn the meat and massage the brine into it at least once a day. When the 12 days have passed, carefully rinse the meat several times. Leave it in a bowl of cold water for half a day. Mince the remaining garlic and dry the meat off. Rub it with the garlic and the rest of the pepper. Preheat the smoker and put the meat inside. Calculate that it will need to stay in there at least 50 minutes for each pound (450 g) of beef. When enough time has passed, check to make sure the internal temperature of the beef has reached 167°F (75°C). Turn off the smoker and let it cool. Sprinkle with more pepper and let it sit in the refrigerator for 2 days, then serve it sliced.

If you don't have much experience, the long marinating time can potentially cause the meat to go bad. To avoid any risks, you can make a simplified version of pastrami which doesn't even call for smoking. Rub the meat with the spices and let it sit in the refrigerator for 1 day (well covered). Then cover it with 1/2 cup (120 ml) of oil, 1/2 cup (120 ml) of vinegar, brown sugar, and allspice. Marinate it in the refrigerator for another 24 hours. Steam it for 2 1/2 hours, keeping the pot covered and occasionally basting with the marinade. Remove the meat from the pot and throw out the water. Line the steamer with aluminum foil and sprinkle it with a layer of brown sugar and spices. Lay the meat on top of it. Cover and cook on low heat for 10 minutes, so that the sugar and spices emit their aromas but don't start to burn. Turn off the heat and let it cool.

CHEESECAKE
UNITED STATES

INGREDIENTS FOR 6 PEOPLE

21 OZ (600 G) CREAM CHEESE

9 OZ (250 G) WHOLE WHEAT SHORTBREAD COOKIES

3/4 CUP + 1 1/2 TBSP (200 ML) SOUR CREAM

10 TBSP (140 G) BUTTER

2/3 CUP + 2 TSP (140 G) SUGAR

1/3 CUP + 1 1/2 TBSP (100 ML) HEAVY CREAM

1/4 CUP (45 G) BROWN SUGAR

2 TBSP (15 G) CORNSTARCH

3 EGGS

HALF A LEMON

1 TSP VANILLA

GROUND CINNAMON

American cheesecake is the last and most famous dessert in a very old tradition based on the use of sweetened cream cheese. It's a favorite in every state of the U.S., but it's especially popular on the East Coast. There are numerous variations in the crust (which can also be made from spongecake), the type of cheese, and the type of cream.

Melt the butter in a double boiler and crush the cookies in a food processor. Mix the crumbs with the butter and brown sugar. You can also add a pinch of cinnamon if you're a fan.
Butter a round springform pan (8 - 9 inches/22 cm) and evenly distribute the mixture over the bottom and sides. Chill it in the refrigerator for 1 hour.
Preheat the oven to 350°F (180°C) and juice the lemon. Mix together the cream cheese, 1/2 cup of sugar, 1/2 teaspoon of vanillin, the cornstarch, and the heavy cream. Add the lemon juice and egg yolks, one at a time. Set aside.
Whip the egg whites into stiff peaks and fold them into the batter.
Pour it over the cookie crumb crust and level it with a spatula. Bake for 30 minutes, then reduce the temperature to 325°F (160°C) and bake it another 30 minutes. Turn off the oven and open the door slightly. Leave the cheesecake in there for about 20 minutes, then remove it and let it cool down to room temperature.
Once it's cooled, make the topping. Mix the rest of the sugar and vanilla with the sour cream. Spread it on the cheesecake and refrigerate it overnight. Alternatively, you can put it in the oven at 350°F (180°C) for a few minutes, let it cool, and refrigerate it for 6 hours. Serve with melted chocolate or berries.

In some versions of the recipe, the eggs are added without beating the whites.
It's a good idea to line the bottom and sides of the pan with parchment paper to keep the cheesecake from sticking; it's not enough to just butter the pan. If you notice that the surface is browning too much after the first 30 minutes of baking, cover it with aluminum foil.

OYSTERS ROCKEFELLER

UNITED STATES

INGREDIENTS FOR 4/6 PEOPLE

24 *BELÓN* OYSTERS (OR *MARENNES-OLERÓN)*

10.5 OZ (300 G) SPINACH (OR WATERCRESS)

7 TBSP (100 G) BUTTER

1 CUP (60 G) BREADCRUMBS

1 CUP (100 G) GRANA PADANO
   OR PARMESAN CHEESE, GRATED

2 TBSP (30 ML) PERNOD (OR OTHER
   ANISE LIQUEUR)

2 CELERY STALKS

2 LEEKS

1 BUNCH OF PARSLEY

1 GARLIC CLOVE

2 TBSP WORCESTERSHIRE SAUCE

1/2 TBSP CHERVIL

1 TSP TABASCO (OR OTHER HOT SAUCE)

LEMON

COARSE SALT

PEPPER

Chef Jules Alciatore, owner of New Orleans restaurant *Antoine*, invented this oyster recipe back in 1899 to replace the specialty of the house at the time. He hadn't been able to serve it for a long time because the main ingredient, snails, had become too scarce.

The new recipe enjoyed great success and the chef decided he would not reveal to anyone the order of ingredients added or the herbs and sauces used. What follows is one of the most reliable "recreations" of the original recipe.

Brush off the oysters and put them in a bowl of salted water, letting them soak and drain for about 6 hours.

Wash and blanch the spinach, then strain it and chop it finely. Mince the parsley, garlic, and chervil. Cut the celery and leeks into very small, thin pieces.

Melt a knob of butter (1 - 2 tablespoons) in a saucepan on low heat (leave the remaining butter out of the refrigerator). Add the celery and leeks. A few minutes later add the garlic, followed immediately by the spinach. Cook for about 10 minutes, still on low heat. Add the breadcrumbs, cheese, Pernod, and sauces. Continue cooking until the mixture has become dry (should take about 5 minutes) and make sure it doesn't stick to the pan.

Transfer to a bowl and add the rest of the butter in thin slices. Then add the parsley and chervil, and season with salt and pepper to taste. Briefly run it through the food processor and let it cool. Meanwhile preheat the oven to 400°F (200°C). Open the oysters and remove them from their shells. Drain away the liquid and set the shells aside.

Sprinkle a layer of coarse salt on the bottom of a baking dish and lay the oyster shells in it. Put an oyster in each one and cover it with a spoonful of the mixture you made earlier. Bake for 5 - 10 minutes and serve with lemon slices.

When it came time to name this new dish, Alciatore decided to name it after billionaire John D. Rockefeller. The sauce he had created was so rich that it was worthy of sharing a name with the era's wealthiest man.

STUFFED THANKSGIVING TURKEY

UNITED STATES

INGREDIENTS FOR 8/10 PEOPLE

1 TURKEY, ABOUT 13 LBS (6 KG)

1 CHICKEN, ABOUT 3 LB (1.3 KG)

2 CUPS (300 G) BREADCRUMBS (OR STALE CUBED
   BREAD)

2/3 CUPS (160 G) BUTTER

6 SAGE LEAVES

2 BELL PEPPERS

2 MEDIUM ONIONS

2 CELERY STALKS

1 SMALL ONION

1 CARROT

1 TBSP OREGANO, CHOPPED

FRESHLY GROUND PEPPER

SALT

A table setting dominated by a roasted, stuffed turkey is the symbol of Thanksgiving, one of the biggest holidays in the U.S. There are countless versions of stuffing, and the following recipe is only one of many possibilities.

Chop the onion and carrot. Then rinse and dry the chicken, and boil it in lots of water with a carrot, celery stalk, and small onion for 50 minutes.
Meanwhile clean out the turkey (and remove the neck if it's still there). Rinse it inside and outside, and leave it in cold water for 30 minutes. Then gently pat it dry with paper towels.
When the chicken is almost done, chop the other celery stalk and the 2 medium onions. Mince the peppers, and sauté all the vegetables in a large pan with half the butter. After a few minutes, add 1 cup (250 ml) of broth from the chicken. Also add the oregano, sage, and salt and pepper to taste. Cook for 5 minutes on medium heat.
Preheat the oven to 350°F (180°C). Transfer the stuffing mixture to a bowl and slowly add the breadcrumbs. Mix well and pour it into a baking dish. Bake for 15 minutes.
Debone the chicken and cut it into small pieces. Add it to the stuffing and bake it for another 30 minutes.
Melt the remaining butter and mix in some salt and pepper. Brush it all over the turkey, inside and out. Carefully fill the cavity with the stuffing, then close the neck and tail with skewers (or sew them). Tie the legs to the tail and firmly attach the wings to the body. Put the turkey in a shallow pan with the breast up and bake at 350°F (180°C). After the first 30 minutes, reduce the temperature to 325°F (160°C). Bake for another 3 hours (time will vary depending on the size of the turkey), basting occasionally with the melted butter.

Another particularly tasty and traditional stuffing is made with 14 ounces (400 g) of chestnuts. In addition to boiled chestnuts, you'll need 2 chopped apples, 2 1/2 tablespoons (20 g) of chopped pine nuts, a turkey heart and liver, and 0.4 lbs (175 g) of chopped lamb.

NEW ENGLAND CLAM CHOWDER

UNITED STATES

INGREDIENTS FOR 4 PEOPLE

4 CUPS (1 L) FISH BROTH

1 LB (450 G) FRESH CLAMS

3/4 CUP + 1 1/2 TBSP (200 ML) WHOLE MILK

3/4 CUP + 1 1/2 TBSP (200 ML) HEAVY CREAM

1/3 LB (150 G) BACON, CUBED

2 TBSP (30 G) BUTTER

1/4 CUP (30 G) FLOUR

2 MEDIUM POTATOES

1 ONION

1 GARLIC CLOVE

EXTRA-VIRGIN OLIVE OIL

SALT

BLACK PEPPER

Clam chowder is a classic American dish. It was brought there in the 19th century by Breton immigrants who settled in the northeast. They made this soup from unsold seafood and other everyday ingredients, like bacon and potatoes. Many variations exist, but New England clam chowder is one of most prominent.

Let the clams drain in fresh salt water for about 3 hours. In the meantime cube the bacon and finely chop the onion. Clean, peel, and dice the potatoes, and sift the flour.
Rinse the clams under running water, scraping them with a small brush and throwing away any that have broken shells. Crush a clove of garlic without peeling it and put it in a pot with a dash of oil. Heat it up and add the clams.
Cover the pot and leave it on medium heat for a few minutes, until the clams open. Shuck at least 2/3 of them and set aside the liquid they cooked in.
Meanwhile heat the fish broth.
In a deep pot, sauté the bacon in the butter. When it gets crispy, remove it and set it on a plate lined with paper towels. Sauté the onion in the same pot. Add the potatoes soon after, followed by the broth. When the potatoes are tender (cooking time will vary depending on their size), season everything with salt and turn off the heat. Add the shucked clams and most of the liquid they cooked in. Pour in the cream, milk, and bacon, then gradually add the flour. Turn the heat back on low and bring it to a boil. Cook for 2 minutes, and add salt to taste. Add the whole clams and let everything sit for a minute. Serve with a garnish of ground pepper to taste.

Other than the New England variety, popular clam chowders in the U.S. include Manhattan, Rhode Island, and Minorcan. Manhattan clam chowder is made with tomato, carrots, and other vegetables instead of milk and cream. Rhode Island clam chowder can be white (with broth) or red (with tomato purée). Minorcan clam chowder is particularly spicy, and is mainly popular in Florida.

WILLIAMSBURG CREAM OF PEANUT SOUP

UNITED STATES

INGREDIENTS FOR 4/6 PEOPLE

4 CUPS (1 L) CHICKEN BROTH
1 CUP (240 ML) HEAVY CREAM
2/3 CUP (160 G) PEANUT BUTTER
1/4 CUP (30 G) ALL-PURPOSE FLOUR
1 3/4 TBSP (25 G) BUTTER

0.7 OZ (20 G) PEANUTS, ABOUT 2 TBSP
1 CELERY STALK
1 SMALL ONION
SALT
BLACK PEPPER

Williamsburg is located in southern Virginia and has a population of just 12,000. Yet it's one of the most famous towns in the United States. Not only is it home to the nation's second oldest university, it has played a very important role in American history and has a number of well-preserved historical sites and materials on display for tourists. This cream of peanut soup is one of the noble hamlet's traditional recipes.

Heat the chicken broth, mince the celery and onion, and chop up the peanuts. Melt the butter in a large pot and sauté the onion and celery for 3 minutes on medium heat. Add the flour and stir for another 2 - 3 minutes. Then add the broth and turn up the heat. Cook for about 15 minutes, stirring frequently. Pass the whole mixture through a sieve (or pureé it in a food processor) and pour the liquid back in the pot. Add the peanut butter and cream. Cook on low heat for 5 minutes, mixing with a whisk. Don't let the mixture reach a boil. Season with salt and pepper to taste and let it cool. Garnish with chopped peanuts and serve. Williamsburg cream of peanut soup is usually an appetizer or side dish, most often served with chicken entrées.

If you want to make a soup with especially intense flavors, increase the amount of peanut butter and slightly reduce the amount of cream. If you want to make it lighter and thinner, add 3 - 7 tablespoons (50 - 100 ml) of milk along with the cream.

CHILI CON CARNE

MEXICO

INGREDIENTS FOR 4 PEOPLE

1 LB (450 G) BEEF

1 CAN (14 OZ/400 G) RED KIDNEY BEANS

2/3 LB (300 G) RIPE TOMATOES, ABOUT 2 1/2
   MEDIUM-SIZED TOMATOES

2/3 CUP (160 ML) BEEF BROTH

2 LARGE ONIONS

2 GARLIC CLOVES

1 - 2 HOT RED PEPPERS

1 BUNCH OF CILANTRO (OR PARSLEY)

4 TBSP EXTRA-VIRGIN OLIVE OIL

1/2 TSP CUMIN

BLACK PEPPER

SALT

The saying, "no man is a prophet in his own land" can be applied to the world of gastronomy as well. The history of *chili con carne*, a savory meat stew that originated in Mexico, is a good example. It's not very popular in Mexico today, but it's found great success just beyond the U.S. border - in Texas. Immigrants in the 19th century started selling it to the people of San Antonio at very low prices. They fell in love with it, and *chili con carne* became a cornerstone of Tex-Mex cooking.

Dice the meat and tomatoes, and mince the hot pepper and cilantro. Peel and chop the garlic and onion.
Heat the hot pepper, garlic, and onion in a pot with the oil. Add the meat and cook it on very high heat for 10 minutes, making sure all sides are browned.
Add the tomato, a sprinkling of pepper, the cilantro, the cumin and a pinch of salt. Mix well and pour in half the broth. Cook on low heat for a little under 30 minutes. Make sure it doesn't stick to the bottom of the pot, and occasionally add a little more broth. In the meantime, open the can of beans and strain them.
When 30 minutes are almost up, add the beans. Let the chili thicken for a few minutes, then turn off the heat and serve it nice and hot.

You can also make chili with ground beef, and some cooks actually prefer to substitute part of the beef with pork. There are varying schools of thought when it comes to the amount of beans (they can be reduced considerably) and the use of tomatoes, which can be replaced with purée or even completely eliminated. Many other ingredients can be added, from bell pepper to a pinch of cinnamon or paprika, lime zest, and even a small piece of bittersweet chocolate.

Difficulty: Medium - Time: 1 hour + cooling time

BURRITOS
MEXICO

INGREDIENTS FOR 4/6 PEOPLE

Tortillas:
3 CUPS + 3 TBSP (400 G) WHEAT FLOUR
1/3 CUP + 1 1/2 TBSP (100 ML) EXTRA-VIRGIN OLIVE OIL
1/4 TSP SALT

Filling:
1/2 LB (200 G) BEEF
1/3 LB (150 G) TILSIT CHEESE (OR MONTEREY JACK)

1/3 LB (150 G) SWEET OR HOT SAUSAGE
3 GARLIC CLOVES
1 - 2 HOT RED PEPPERS
1 ONION
4 TBSP EXTRA-VIRGIN OLIVE OIL
2 TBSP CILANTRO
2 TBSP CANNED CORN
PEPPER

Also called tacos de *harina, burritos* are flour tortillas filled with meat. They're typical of northeastern Mexico, near the U.S. border. Melted cheese, sauces, and various vegetables might be added to the meat (which can be beef, pork, or chicken).

Sift the flour, add the salt, and create a well. Pour in the oil and mix everything together. Add 3/4 cup (175 ml) of warm water, 1 tablespoon at a time.
Mix for 5 minutes and form a long, thin cylinder. Let the dough rest for 15 minutes under a clean towel. Divide it into pieces just a little bigger than a walnut (or larger if you prefer bigger tortillas). Let it rest for another 10 minutes. Flatten the dough pieces into discs. Heat a nonstick pan and cook the tortillas one by one on medium heat, flipping them when the surface starts to bubble. Cook for just 1 minute, then remove them from the pan and set them aside.
Peel and crush the garlic. Strain the corn, dice the cheese, and chop the cilantro, hot pepper, and onion. Cut the sausage and beef into small pieces. Heat the oil in a pan and place each tortilla inside for a few seconds, softening them on both sides.
In the same oil sauté the onion, garlic, chili pepper, and cilantro. Add the beef and sausage, season with salt and pepper to taste, and cover the pan. Cook on low heat for 15 minutes, adding 1 or more tablespoons of water (and/or tomato purée) if the meat is getting too dry. When it's almost done, add the corn and preheat the oven to 400°F (200°C). Spoon some of the meat mixture onto each tortilla, spreading it across the center. Add a few pieces of cheese and roll up the *burritos*, folding in the sides. Lay them in a baking dish and sprinkle with more cheese. Bake them for a few minutes and serve.

In Spanish, burrito *means "little donkey". According to tradition, these filled tortillas got their name because the man who invented them, Juan Mendez di Ciudad Juárez, did not sell them only in his own town. He also sold them in nearby El Paso (Texas), where he traveled on the back of a donkey.*

GUACAMOLE

MEXICO

INGREDIENTS FOR 4 PEOPLE

2 RIPE AVOCADOS

1 - 2 TOMATOES

1 - 2 GREEN CHILIES

1 SPRIG OF CILANTRO

1 SMALL WHITE ONION

1 GARLIC CLOVE

HALF A LIME

BLACK PEPPER

SALT

Avocado, lime, and salt. Once upon a time these were the only ingredients in guacamole, a Mexican dip whose name reveals its Pre-Columbian origins. It derives from the word *ahuacatl*, which means "avocado" in the Aztec language. This specialty has been enhanced with the addition of other flavors over the centuries, and today it's the perfect partner for tacos and tortillas. Warning: tradition dictates that you should never use a blender or food processor when making guacamole because it would break up the avocado pulp too much.

Clean and mince the garlic and onion. Mince the cilantro as well. Slice the chilies into small pieces and dice the tomato, removing the skin and seeds.

Clean the avocados, cut them in half, and remove the pits. Scoop out the pulp and cut it into small pieces. Put them in a large bowl or mortar, and mash with a fork or pestle until they're creamy. If you prefer a chunkier dip, mash only half the pulp and set the rest aside.

Combine the mashed avocado with half the cilantro and all the other vegetables. Squeeze half a lime and add the juice, followed by lots of freshly ground pepper (one variation also calls for the lime zest). If you chose not to mash all the avocado, now is the time to add the pieces you set aside. Add a pinch of salt and stir carefully. Sprinkle with the remaining cilantro, cover, and let it sit for at least 30 minutes before serving.

A dip much like guacamole (and erroneously called by the same name) has become a Tex-Mex standard. Though it appears to be similar to the original, it has a decidedly different taste. It includes mayonnaise and sour cream, which can make it hard to fully appreciate the avocado flavor.

PLATANOS EN TENTACIÓN

CUBA

INGREDIENTS FOR 4 PEOPLE

3 - 4 *PLATANOS* (PLANTAINS) OR 6 UNRIPE BANANAS

1/2 CUP (100 G) PACKED BROWN SUGAR

2 TBSP (30 G) BUTTER

HALF A LIME

2 TBSP GROUND CINNAMON

2 TBSP RUM (OR SHERRY)

Platanos en tentación are caramelized bananas. The original recipe calls for plantains, not the ordinary yellow bananas that dominate supermarkets. Plantains are larger, less sweet, and more fibrous than bananas, and they're only eaten cooked.

Zest half the lime. Peel the plantains and slice them into 1 1/2 inch (4 cm) pieces. Heat the butter in a heavy-bottomed pan and sauté the plantains on low heat until they start to turn golden brown on both sides. Pour in enough water to cover them up halfway, then add the cinnamon, lime zest, rum, and sugar. Mix well and let the liquid thicken for about 5 minutes, then turn off the heat. *Platanos en tentación* are served with boiled rice.

Another cooking method calls for removing the plantain pieces from the pan as soon as they start to brown on both sides, and placing them on a plate lined with paper towels. Then you mash some of them with a meat tenderizer and melt the sugar in a small pot. Pour in the rum and lime zest, and stir on medium heat. Add the cinnamon and 1 cup of water. Let the mixture thicken, then put all the partially fried plantain pieces in the pot. Cook for a couple of minutes, add another knob of butter (about 1 - 2 tablespoons), stir, and serve.

JERK CHICKEN

JAMAICA

INGREDIENTS FOR 4 PEOPLE

1 CHICKEN, CUT IN HALF

4 GARLIC CLOVES

4 FRESH SCOTCH BONNET CHILI PEPPERS
  (OR *HABANEROS*)

3 SHALLOTS (OR SPRING ONIONS)

1 ONION

HALF A LIME

2 TBSP EXTRA-VIRGIN OLIVE OIL

2 TBSP SOY SAUCE

1 TBSP SUGAR (BROWN SUGAR IS BEST)

1 TBSP FRESH THYME

2 TSP ALLSPICE

2 TSP BLACK PEPPER

1/2 TSP GROUND CINNAMON

1/2 TSP GROUND GINGER

1/2 TSP GROUND NUTMEG

SALT

Jerk is a traditional Jamaican spice mix, hot sauce, and cooking method. Meat is rubbed with the spices or marinated in the sauce, then cooked on the grill. The grill racks are still placed over metal barrels in many parts of Jamaica, just as they were a century ago. This way the meat takes on a smoky flavor, and the coal or wood is enhanced with fragrant berries. However, the oven often replaces this more traditional cooking method.

Clean and roughly chop the shallots and onion. Juice the lime, peel the garlic, and remove the seeds from the hot peppers. Put everything in a blender or food processor with the salt, spices, sugar, oil, and soy sauce. Blend until the ingredients are combined into a smooth sauce, then spread it on the chicken and let it marinate in the refrigerator for at least 4 hours (according to tradition it's best to marinate the chicken overnight). Take the chicken out of the refrigerator and remove it from the marinade. Keep it at room temperature for about 1 hour and preheat the oven to 400°F (200°C) or light the grill.
If you're using the oven, put the chicken in a wide pan with the skin side up and bake it for about 30 minutes. Then flip it over and put it back in the oven for at least 20 minutes (cooking time can vary quite a bit depending on the size of the chicken).
If you're using the grill, start cooking the chicken with the skin side down and don't turn it over until the skin gets crispy. Occasionally brush the chicken with the marinade.
Don't worry if the outside of the chicken is blackened - sometimes the jerk chicken served in Jamaica actually looks carbonized. The important thing is that the meat stays tender.

Remember that scotch bonnet and habanero *peppers are very hot. If you're not used to such spiciness, you can substitute them with another less "aggressive" variety.*
You can substitute (or combine) the oil in the marinade with 2 tablespoons of dark rum and the juice of half an orange. You can also increase the amounts sugar and allspice. The latter, also known as "Jamaica pepper" or "pimenta", is one of the most prominent ingredients in Caribbean cuisine.

GRIOT

HAITI

Difficulty: Difficult - Time: 1 hour + marinating time

INGREDIENTS FOR 4 PEOPLE

2LBS (900 G) PORK (SHOULDER IS BEST)

2 SOUR ORANGES

1 PLANTAIN (*PLATANO*) OR TWO UNRIPE BANANAS

1 LIME

1 GREEN CHILI PEPPER

1 SHALLOT (OR HALF AN ONION)

1 GARLIC CLOVE

1 TBSP CHIVES

1/2 TBSP PARSLEY

THYME

VEGETABLE OIL

GREEN PEPPER

SALT

Haitian cooking is very fond of mixing flavors. It has a fragrant, spiced aroma, but is rarely hot and spicy. Made with meat marinated in citrus juice and served with fried plantains, *griot* is emblematic of this style.

Cube the pork, rinse it, and pat it dry. Juice the lime and oranges, then mince and mix the chives, thyme, and parsley.
Mince the garlic and shallot too. Put the meat in a bowl with the citrus juices, a pinch of salt and green pepper, the entire chili pepper, and all the minced herbs. Mix well and let it marinate in the refrigerator for at least 2 hours (the ideal would be to marinate it for half a day).
Remove the meat from the bowl and let the excess marinade drip off. Then put it in a pot and cover it with water. Simmer on medium-low heat for 45 minutes. Stir occasionally and eventually top it off with more water. When the simmering time is almost up, peel the plantains and cut them into rounds about 1/4 - 1/2 inch (1 cm) thick. Soak them in a saltwater bath for a few minutes, then dry them.
Remove the meat with a slotted spoon and transfer it to a large skillet with a bit of oil. It's important that it be heavy-bottomed so the heat will be evenly distributed. Fry the pork on low heat until all the pieces have browned.
At the same time, fry the plantains in a separate pan. After 2 minutes, turn off the heat and remove the plantain slices. Lay them on paper towels for a minute, then mash them with a meat tenderizer. Turn the heat back on and fry the plantains for another 2 - 3 minutes, then remove them and soak up the excess oil with paper towels. Arrange them on a serving plate with the hot pork. Serve with meat, boiled rice and a sprinkling of grated ginger.

If you don't particularly care for sweet and sour flavors, you can quickly rinse the cubed pork after you take it out of the marinade and before you cook it. Doing so will make the lime, herb, and orange flavors more subtle.

JAMBALAYA
FRENCH ANTILLES

INGREDIENTS FOR 4 PEOPLE

5 CUPS (1.2 L) BEEF BROTH

1 LB (450 G) TOMATOES, ABOUT 4 MEDIUM-SIZED
   TOMATOES

1 LB (450 G) CHICKEN BREAST, CUT INTO PIECES

1 LB (450 G) HOT SAUSAGE

2 CUPS + 2 TBSP (400 G) PARBOILED RICE

2 GARLIC CLOVES

2 BAY LEAVES

1 BELL PEPPER

1 ONION

2 TSP BLACK PEPPER

1 TSP WHITE PEPPER

1 HOT RED PEPPER

1 TSP THYME

EXTRA-VIRGIN OLIVE OIL

SALT

Popular in most of the Antilles, as well as New Orleans and other parts of the American South, jambalaya is a sort of a Creole reinterpretation of Spanish *paella*. Much like its illustrious European cousin, there are infinite adaptations and it can be made with meat or shellfish. The name "jambalaya" supposedly comes from the French word *jambon* ("ham"), one of the ingredients that might be included in the recipe. What follows is only one of the numerous variations on this dish; it has chicken and sausage, but no ham.

Heat the broth and cut the bell pepper and sausage into small pieces. Mince the hot pepper and dice the chicken breast and tomatoes.
Peel and chop the garlic and onion. Sauté them with a bit of oil, and after 2 minutes add the bell pepper and tomatoes. Stir for another 2 - 3 minutes, then add the chicken and sausage along with a ladleful of broth. Season with hot pepper, bay leaves, thyme, and half the pepper. Sauté on high heat until the meat is browned on all sides, then pour in the rest of the broth. Add the remaining pepper and season with salt to taste. Now add the rice, starting in the middle and working quickly and uniformly toward the edges. At this point do not stir anymore. Let it cook on medium-high heat for 8 minutes, then reduce the heat and wait for the broth to absorb (it should take another 10 - 12 minutes). If the broth starts evaporating too quickly, add a bit of water and cover the pan. Let it sit for a minute and bring it to the table.

Depending on personal preferences, you can add other vegetables to the mix before serving, especially finely chopped carrots, celery, spring onion, and a few parsley leaves. You can also add more flavor with 2 tablespoons of tomato purée, which should be added together with the bell pepper.

EMPANADAS ANTIOQUEÑAS

COLOMBIA

INGREDIENTS FOR 6 PEOPLE

3 CUPS (500 G) FRESH CORN KERNELS

1 LB (450 G) POTATOES

1 LB (450 G) CHOPPED MEAT (BEEF IS BEST)

1/2 CUP (120 ML) HOGAO SAUCE

2 TBSP DARK BROWN SUGAR

2 TBSP CORNSTARCH

1 TSP CUMIN

OIL FOR FRYING

EXTRA-VIRGIN OLIVE OIL

SALT

GROUND PEPPER

Empanadas are tasty stuffed pastries popular throughout South America. From one country to another (and from one region to another within each country) there are differences in size, flours used for the dough, and ingredients for the filling. Those made in the Department of Antioquia in northwestern Colombia are famous for the delicate taste of their dough, which is made from corn, as well as their meat and potato filling.

Rinse and drain the corn, then boil it in a pot of water. Cooking time will differ based on the "age" of the kernels. On average 10 minutes should be enough, but make sure they are tender before you turn off the heat.

Peel and dice the potatoes, and boil them in another pot with salted water.

Strain the potatoes and corn separately, then mince the corn well and combine it with the sugar, cornstarch, and a bit of salt.

Drizzle some oil in a pot and sauté the meat, seasoning with *hogao* sauce and cumin. After 10 minutes, add the potatoes and pour in 4 cups (1 L) of water. Cover and simmer on low heat for 25 minutes, stirring occasionally.

Meanwhile form the corn mixture into little balls. Flatten them with the palm of your hand until you have thin discs.

Put a spoonful of filling in the center of each disc and fold them into half-moons, sealing the edges well. Then pinch around the edges to make little decorative folds.

Heat enough oil to fry them in a large skillet. Fry the *empanadas* until the dough turns golden brown. Then drain away the excess oil, sprinkle with pepper, and serve.

Hogao *sauce is made from onion and tomato, and it's especially popular in Colombia. Oregano, saffron, cumin, and pepper are some of the spices that might be used to flavor it.*

AJIACO

COLOMBIA

INGREDIENTS FOR 6 PEOPLE

1 LB (450 G) CREOLE POTATOES
1/2 LB (225 G) WHITE POTATOES
1/2 LB (225 G) YELLOW POTATOES
3 CHICKEN BREASTS
3 FRESH EARS OF CORN
3 GARLIC CLOVES
HALF AN ONION
SALT

The term *ajiaco* can refer to two difference plates in Latin America—one is Cuban and the other is Colombian. The Cuban dish is made with spiced pork, while the Colombian dish that follows is a chicken, corn, and potato soup. It's made with many different recipes throughout Colombia: in some cases the chicken breasts are replaced with other cuts of chicken, while in others the corn and potatoes are boiled with the meat. Some don't even call for marinating in the refrigerator overnight; they simply add garlic and onion (and eventually other flavors) to the broth.

Crush the garlic and mince the onion. Mix them together and add a bit of salt.
Rub the mixture into the chicken breasts, then refrigerate them in a covered bowl overnight.
Add the chicken breasts to a pot of water, season with salt, and boil for about 10 minutes (or longer if they're very large). Meanwhile wash the ears of corn and cut them in half (or you prefer, you can slice the kernels off). Clean and peel the potatoes, cutting the smallest ones in half and cutting the rest into slices about 1/8 - 1/4 inch (0.5 cm) thick.
When the chicken breasts are tender, remove them from the pot. Cut them into thin strips about 1 inch (1 - 3 cm) long and put them in a bowl. Use the broth from the chicken to boil the potatoes and corn. If necessary, add more water. When the potatoes start to break up, turn off the heat. Transfer it all to a large bowl and mix thoroughly. Distribute the soup among individual serving bowls and serve hot. The most traditional sides are sliced avocado, hot salsa, and a cream and caper sauce.

The secret to good ajiaco *is the type of potato. It's important to use at least three kinds that have different tastes and consistencies. Colombian Creole potatoes are difficult to find at supermarkets, and can be replaced with another sweet potato variety.*

CREMA DE JOJOTO
VENEZUELA

INGREDIENTS FOR 4 PEOPLE

8 1/2 CUPS (2 L) BEEF BROTH

2 CUPS + 2 TBSP (500 ML) MILK

5 FRESH EARS OF CORN

2 SHALLOTS

1 BUNCH OF PARSLEY

2 TBSP BUTTER

SALT

Corn, the most American of grains, plays a very large role in Venezuelan cooking. *Crema de jojoto*, a simple yet tasty soup, is the dish that best utilizes soft, fresh corn.

Heat the broth and slice the kernels off the ears of corn. Chop the parsley and shallots. Set aside 1/5 of the kernels (choose the softest, smallest ones) and put the rest in a food processor on medium speed. Once they've broken down well, gradually add the milk and continue to blend, but not too fast.
Heat 1 tablespoon of butter in a pot and sear the shallot. Add the blended corn mixture. Slowly pour in all the broth, stirring continuously. Add salt to taste and cook on low heat. Mix it with a wooden spoon, and when the soup starts to thicken add the kernels you set aside. When 20 minutes have passed since it started cooking, add the rest of the butter and the parsley. Cook for 1 more minute to let the flavors come together, then turn off the heat and serve it hot.

The main variation on this recipe concerns the shallot and parsley, which can also be added direct-
ly to the broth while it's heating. If you choose to do so, you don't have to use another pot and
you'll need only 1 tablespoon of butter. Pour the blended corn mixture right into the broth and
use the butter only to bring it all together.

PABELLON CRIOLLO

VENEZUELA

INGREDIENTS FOR 4 PEOPLE

1 LB (450 G) BEEF

7 OZ (200 G) DRY BLACK BEANS, ABOUT 1 CUP

1 CUP (190 G) BASMATI RICE

1/3 CUP (80 G) SMOKED BACON, CHOPPED

2 GARLIC CLOVES

1 1/4 LARGE BELL PEPPER

1 PLANTAIN (*PLATANO*)

1 TOMATO

1 CARROT

1 LARGE ONION

1 SMALL ONION

1 DRIED HOT RED PEPPER

EXTRA-VIRGIN OLIVE OIL

SALT

PEPPER

Pabellón criollo is a single dish divided into several parts. It includes beef, boiled rice, legumes, and plantains. Traditionally, the three main ingredients represent the diverse ethnic groups of Venezuela. Meat is amber brown like the indigenous peoples, rice is white like the Europeans, and the legumes are black like the Venezuelans of African origin.

Rinse the beans and soak them overnight, then strain them and boil them for 1 hour. Strain them again and set aside 2/3 cup (160 ml) of the water they cooked in.
Meanwhile, put the meat in a pressure cooker with a little bit of water for 30 minutes. Then turn it off and let the meat cool, setting aside about 2/3 cup (160 ml) of broth. Chop up a clove of garlic, the larger onion, the hot pepper, and the carrot. Dice the tomato and 1 bell pepper. When the meat has cooled, cut it into long, thin slices. Sauté it in a pan with a bit of oil and the chopped vegetables. If necessary add the broth you saved (another version also calls for 1 tablespoon of tomato purée). Season with salt and pepper and cook for 10 minutes, making sure nothing sticks to the pan.
Chop up the small onion and dice the remaining 1/4 bell pepper. Cook them in a pan with a bit of oil, then add the beans, bacon, and the water previously set aside. Season with salt and pepper, and cook until the mixture thickens (if the beans still aren't tender, add some more water and cook a little longer).
Mince the last garlic clove. Rinse and strain the rice. Heat the garlic in a pot with some oil, then add the rice and a pinch of salt. Cook on medium heat and add 2 cups (475 ml) of water. When it starts to boil, reduce the heat to the lowest setting. Cover and cook until all the water is absorbed.
Peel the plantain and slice it into rounds about 1/4 - 1/2 inch (1 cm) thick. Fry the slices in a pan with just a little bit of oil. After 2 minutes, turn off the heat and remove the plantain pieces. Lay them briefly on paper towels, then mash them. Turn the heat back on and fry them for another 2 - 3 minutes. Remove them and let them sit on paper towels for a minute. Then arrange them on a serving plate next to the meat, beans, and rice.

FEIJOADA
À BRASILEIRA

BRAZIL

INGREDIENTS FOR 4/6 PEOPLE

14 OZ (400 G) DRY BLACK BEANS, ABOUT 2 CUPS

2/3 LB (300 G) PORK RIBS

1/4 LB (113 G) SWEET SAUSAGE

1/4 LB (113 G) HOT SAUSAGE

1/4 LB (113 G) FRESH BACON

1/4 LB (113 G) SMOKED BACON

3 BAY LEAVES

2 - 3 GARLIC CLOVES

2 HOT RED PEPPERS, DRIED

1 PIG EAR

1 PIG FOOT

1 PIG TAIL

1 - 2 TBSP BUTTER

1 CELERY STALK

HALF AN ONION

2 TBSP FLOUR

EXTRA-VIRGIN OLIVE OIL

SALT - PEPPER

The beans can be black or brown, depending on whether you choose the Rio de Janeiro version or the Bahia version. The ratio of beans to pork can also change significantly. The cuts of pork can vary from one region of Brazil to another (other cuts of pork might replace the ribs, and you can add the tongue or substitute it for the ear) and some versions include beef. Different areas also use different herbs and spices. Brazilian *feijoada* (from *feijão*, meaning "beans") is therefore a recipe that's difficult to set in stone. The following is only one of many interpretations.

Rinse the beans and soak them in a bowl of water with 1 bay leaf for half a day. Then strain them and set aside. Chop up the bacon and sausages. Scald the foot, tail, and ear for 10 minutes to eliminate some of their fat. Put the beans in a large pot with some oil. Add the scalded pieces, along with the rest of the meat and the remaining 2 bay leaves. Cover everything with cold water, season with salt and pepper to taste, and simmer for 1 1/2 hours on medium-low heat. Meanwhile chop the onion and celery, and peel the garlic. Add them to the pot and cook for at least another 30 minutes.

Then put the meat, beans, and most of the broth in single-serving earthenware bowls or one deep serving bowl.

Chop the hot peppers and sauté them with the butter, gradually pouring in the flour. Stir continuously and add 1 1/4 cups (300 ml) of the remaining broth from the pot. Let it thicken and pour it over the meat and vegetables.

Serve the *feijoada* hot with boiled rice, vegetables, orange wedges, and cold beer.

One version of the recipe concerns the cooking method. The bacon can first be cooked in a frying pan with garlic, hot pepper, onion, and some of the water from boiling the beans. After a few minutes, it can be added to the big pot with the rest of the ingredients. In this case, it's not necessary to add the mix of flour and hot peppers at the end.

Difficulty: Medium - Time: 2 hours 30 minutes + soaking time

CHURRASCO

BRAZIL

INGREDIENTS FOR 6 PEOPLE

1 1/3 LBS (600 G) SIRLOIN STEAK

2/3 LB (300 G) MIXED SAUSAGES (BEEF AND PORK)

3 TBSP WINE VINEGAR

COARSE SALT

SALT

Churrasco is a traditional dish from the State of Rio Grande do Sul in southern Brazil (bordered by Argentina and Uruguay). At one time it was only made with beef, but today it's made with many types of meat including chicken, turkey, pork, and sometimes even lamb.

Cube the steak, then drizzle it with the vinegar and sprinkle with coarse salt. Let it marinate for 1 hour. In the meantime get a fire started for barbecuing, preferably using wood with no chemical additives. Spear the steak cubes onto six large skewers (or 12 small ones), alternating with the sausages. Place the grate about 20 inches (50 cm) from the fire and grill the skewers. If you prefer your *churrasco* with a particularly smoky flavor, raise the grate higher. If you prefer a "cleaner" taste place it closer to the fire, but don't let it touch the flames.

Cooking times will vary depending on taste, the size of the meat pieces, and the position of the grate. Add salt to taste and serve with lots of white rice.

Besides sirloin steak, one of the most common cuts of meat for churrasco *is* picanha, *top sirloin cap steak. If you want to substitute this or add it to the other meats, sprinkle it with coarse salt and let it sit for an hour. Then clean it well and cut it into slices about 2 - 3 inches (6 - 8 cm) thick. Skewer the slices, folding them over to create a slight curve and piercing through the fat around them. It's important to leave the fat on because it will dissolve and leave the meat particularly tender and flavorful.*

BACALHAU À BAIANA

BRAZIL

INGREDIENTS FOR 4 PEOPLE

1 LB (450G) SALTED DRIED COD

3/4 CUP + 1 1/2 TBSP (200 ML) DENSE COCONUT MILK

1 ONION

1 SHALLOT

1 GARLIC CLOVE

1 TOMATO

1 RED BELL PEPPER

1 GREEN BELL PEPPER

1 FRESH GREEN CHILI PEPPER

1 SPRIG OF PARSLEY

4 TBSP EXTRA-VIRGIN OLIVE OIL

2 TBSP PALM OIL (OR SEEDS)

SALT

PEPPER

Brazil was long dominated by the Portuguese, who brought many specialties from their own gastronomic traditions. One of these is *bacalhau* (salted dried cod), which became the fundamental ingredient in a particularly delectable dish from the State of Bahia. The adjective *baiana* actually means "Bahia style".

Soak the cod in cold water for at least 24 hours (change the water occasionally). Drain and clean it, removing all the skin and bones. Thoroughly pat it dry with paper towels and cut it into pieces about 2 inches (5 cm) wide.
Slice the onion, dice the tomato, and crush the garlic. Cut the bell peppers into strips and the chili pepper into rounds, discarding the seeds.
Heat the palm oil and olive oil in a terracotta pot. Add the onion, garlic, bell peppers, and chili pepper. Stir them together and cook for a few minutes until softened. Then add the tomato and the cod. Pour in 1 cup + 1 tablespoon of hot water and cover the pot.
Simmer on low heat for 10 minutes, checking to make sure it doesn't stick to the bottom. Chop the shallot and the parsley. When 10 minutes is up, add them along with the coconut milk. Stir to combine and cook for another few minutes (use a fork to check if the fish is done). Add salt and pepper to taste, then serve with potatoes and white rice.

One of the most common side dishes in Brazil is farofa, *made with cassava or millet flour. The flour is cooked with oil (in the State of Bahia they use palm oil) and other ingredients, which vary depending on the main dish being served with the* farofa. *They could be herbs and vegetables (to go with fish, like cod), pieces of meat, or banana slices.*

DOCE JERIMUM COM COCO

BRAZIL

INGREDIENTS FOR 4/6 PEOPLE
1 PUMPKIN, 3 LBS (1.3 KG)
2 1/2 CUPS (500 G) SUGAR
2/3 CUP (50 G) COCONUT FLAKES
GROUND CINNAMON
CLOVES

The name means "pumpkin and coconut dessert". All that's added to those ingredients is water, a few spices (usually cloves and cinnamon), and sugar. The amount of sugar varies according to personal taste and the natural sweetness of the pumpkin. The amount listed here is a version that tends to favor the main ingredients and limit the rest, but in some particularly sweet versions there might be as much as a teaspoon of sugar for every ounce (28 g) of pumpkin (without seeds and rind).

Remove the pumpkin rind and seeds, and dice the pulp. Put it in a pot, cover it with water, and boil it on low heat for 25 minutes. Then strain it and mash it with a fork until it reaches a creamy consistency (it's best not to use a food processor because it would be too aggressive for the pumpkin pulp).
Put the mashed pumpkin in a smaller pot and add the sugar. Bring it back to a boil, stirring well. Then add the coconut and 2 - 3 cloves. Mix well and leave it on low heat for 5 minutes. It's important to make sure the pumpkin doesn't stick to the bottom of the pot.
Turn off the heat, let it cool, and serve it in individual bowls with a sprinkling of cinnamon on top.

The taste of coconut and cloves can easily overpower the very delicate pumpkin flavor, so this recipe limits them to a few teaspoons. If you particularly love the taste of these ingredients, you can increase the quantities and add them to the pumpkin pureé as soon as it goes back on the stove, instead of 5 minutes before turning off the heat. This will fully release all their flavors.

TUNA CEVICHE
PERU

INGREDIENTS FOR 4 PEOPLE

1 LB (450G) TUNA
2 - 3 LIMES
1 CHILI PEPPER
1 GARLIC CLOVE
HALF A RED ONION

HALF A CUCUMBER
HALF A BELL PEPPER
CILANTRO LEAVES
SALT

Ceviche (or *chebiche*) is raw fish or shellfish marinated in lime juice. Tuna is one of the fish that lends itself best to this preparation technique.

Though *ceviche* has been popular throughout western Latin America for some time, it is most associated with the country of Perú and was already being eaten there in the Pre-Columbian era (at the time, fruit juices other than lime were used).

Mince the garlic and chili pepper and mix them together with a pinch of salt. Squeeze the limes into a bowl. Rinse the tuna and cut it into cubes or very thin slices. Season it with the garlic and chili pepper mix.

Marinate the tuna in the bowl of lime juice, making sure it is fully covered in the liquid. Put it in the refrigerator for at least 30 minutes. While it's marinating, slice the red onion very thinly and mince the cucumber and bell pepper. Mix the vegetables together. When you take the tuna out of the refrigerator, spread the vegetable mix evenly on top and let it sit at room temperature for 15 minutes. Garnish with a few cilantro leaves (or parsley) and serve it with the marinade.

In addition to the above ingredients, ceviche de atún *lends itself well to fruit-based variations of the recipe. To make it with fruit, marinate the tuna without the first step of seasoning with garlic and chili pepper. Instead of onion and bell pepper, use a minced mango and passion fruit pulp. To season, grate a small piece of ginger and sprinkle a bit of ground white pepper.*

CAZUELA DE AVE

CHILE

INGREDIENTS FOR 4/6 PEOPLE

1 WHOLE CHICKEN (3 LBS/1.3 KG), ALREADY DIVIDED
  INTO PIECES
4 CUPS (1 L) CHICKEN BROTH
1/2 LB (225 G) PUMPKIN, JUST OVER TWO CUPS
  CUBED
1 CUP (200 G) RICE
8 SMALL POTATOES
2 EARS OF FRESH CORN

1 ONION
1 CARROT
1 CELERY STALK
1 GARLIC CLOVE
1 BUNCH OF PARSLEY (OR CILANTRO)
OREGANO
SALT
PEPPER

Cazuela de ave is a chicken and corn soup that can be made in many different ways, adding or eliminating various ingredients. For example, you can leave out the pumpkin and add about 2 cups (225 g) of green beans, a few cabbage leaves, and half a bell pepper. You can also substitute a small, light pasta for the rice.

Rinse and dry the chicken. Break the ears of corn in half, peel the garlic and potatoes, and slice the carrot into rounds. Remove the pumpkin rind and seeds, and cut it into small pieces. Mince the parsley, slice the onion, and heat the broth.
Pour plenty of olive oil into a large saucepan. As soon as it's lukewarm, add the chicken, garlic, onion, carrot, and celery. Then add a pinch of oregano, salt, and pepper. When the chicken starts to brown, pour in the broth and let it cook for 5 minutes. Add the corn, rice, pumpkin, and potatoes. Let it cook another 20 minutes, stirring occasionally. Then turn the heat off and let it sit for a few minutes. Sprinkle with parsley and serve it hot.

If you notice that the chicken is not cooked yet, but the pumpkin and/or potato pieces are about to fall apart, remove them from the pot and set them aside, and continue to cook the chicken. Return them to the pot just before you turn off the heat.

ASADO
ARGENTINA

INGREDIENTS FOR 6 PEOPLE

3.3 LBS (1.5 KG) BEEF (SHORT RIBS, FLANK STEAK,
    SWEETBREADS, AND KIDNEYS)
1.1 LBS (500 G) BLOOD SAUSAGE AND MIXED SAUSAGE
    (BEEF AND PORK)
3 TBSP WHITE WINE VINEGAR
SALT

Chimichurri
4 TBSP EXTRA-VIRGIN OLIVE OIL
4 TBSP WHITE WINE VINEGAR
4 TBSP PARSLEY
1 GARLIC CLOVE
1 TSP OREGANO
1 TSP BLACK PEPPER
1 TSP SALT

When you hear the word "Argentina" it immediately brings to mind herds of livestock and the highest quality beef. Asado is simply barbecued meat, which is usually made on the grill (or *parilla*). Alternative cooking methods do exist, such as the use of large spits planted right in the ground or holes dug under a barbecue pit. However you cook it, you can't have *asado* without short ribs, entrails, *chorizo fresco* (sausage) and *chimichurri*, a sauce that varies greatly depending on regional and family traditions.

Make the *chimichurri* first. Combine all the ingredients in a food processor and blend well. Transfer it to a bowl and let it sit for 3 - 4 hours.
Get the barbecue fire going (preferably using wood without any chemical additives) and start with the ribs, placing them bone side down. Increase the heat after 15 minutes and cook until the meat takes on a nice color. Turn them over, season with salt, and cook slowly until the fat dissolves. Soon after you've turned the ribs, season the flank steak with salt and place it on the grill. As with the ribs, turn over the flank steak when it takes on a nice color.
In the meantime, pour the vinegar into a bowl. Dilute it with a little bit of water and add a pinch of salt. Clean the kidney and cut it into slices about 1/2 inch (just over 1 cm) thick. Marinate it in the vinegar solution for 30 minutes. Rinse the sweetbreads and let them dry. Slice them the same way as the kidney, but don't marinate them.
Prick the mixed sausages with a fork and put them on the grill. About 15 minutes before the ribs are done, add the blood sausages. After another 10 minutes add the kidney and sweetbreads, which take a very short time to cook (the slices do need to be grilled on both sides). One by one, as they're ready, serve the kidneys, sweetbreads, mixed sausages, and blood sausages. It's not necessary to present everything together on one large plate, in fact the meat is usually brought to the table last.
Serve everything with *chimichurri* and a mixed salad or grilled corn on the cob.

Cooking times vary depending on the intensity of the heat and the sizes of various cuts of meat. In any case, it's important to ensure that the asado *cooking process is long and slow.*

DULCE DE LECHE
ARGENTINA

INGREDIENTS FOR 4 PEOPLE
3 QUARTS (3 L) FRESH WHOLE MILK
5 CUPS (1 KG) SUGAR
1 VANILLA BEAN
1/2 TSP BAKING SODA

The taste of this milk caramel is similar to toffee, and the density can vary considerably based on cooking time. *Dulce de leche* can be served as a dessert, spread on bread, or used as a topping for ice cream and cakes.

Slice open the vanilla bean lengthwise. Pour the sugar into a pot (copper and aluminum are best) with 2 quarts + 3 cups (2750 ml) of milk. Heat it, add the vanilla bean, and mix until the sugar has dissolved. Meanwhile dissolve the baking soda in the remaining cup of milk. When the sugar mixture starts to boil, remove it from the heat and add the milk with dissolved baking soda. Mix well and put the pot back on the stove over low heat. Let it simmer and thicken for about 1 1/2 hours, stirring occasionally with a wooden spoon (in the final phase of cooking you have to stir continuously so the sweet mixture doesn't stick to the bottom of the pot). When it reaches the desired consistency, turn off the heat and transfer the dulce de leche to small single-serving bowls. Serve it cold.

There's also a faster way to make dulce de leche, though it's frowned upon by purists (and allows no control over sweetness and density). Just put a closed can of condensed milk into a pressure cooker and fully cover it with water.
Cook for 25 minutes from when the pot starts whistling, then let it cool and open the can.

RECIPE INDEX

INGREDIENTS INDEX

PHOTO CREDITS

Page 1 Sprint/Photolibrary.com
Pages 2-3 Robertson, Lew/Stock Food/Olycom
Page 4 Blin/Sucrè Salè/Tips Images
Page 5 Blin/Sucrè Salè/Tips Images
Page 15 Lippmann/Sucrè Salè/Tips Images
Page 17 FoodPhotogr.Eising/Stock Food/Olycom
Page 19 Winkelmann, Bernhard/Stock Food/Olycom
Page 21 Leser, Nicolas/Stock Food/Olycom
Page 23 Adam/Sucrè Salè/Tips Images
Page 25 Hall/Sucrè Salè/Tips Images
Page 27 Leser, Nicolas/Stock Food/Olycom
Page 29 Vasseur, Frederic/Stock Food/Olycom
Page 31 Hussenot/Sucrè Salè/Tips Images
Page 33 FoodPhotogr.Eising/Stock Food/Olycom
Page 35 Vasseur, Frederic/Stock Food/Olycom
Page 37 Nilsson, P./Stock Food/Olycom
Page 39 Chris Bayley/Photolibrary.com
Page 41 Patrice de Villiers/Photolibrary.com
Page 43 Teubner Foodfoto/Stock Food/Olycom
Page 45 Hall/Sucrè Salè/Tips Images
Page 47 Jacobs, Martin/Stock Food/Olycom
Page 49 Studio Schiermann/Stock Food/Olycom
Page 51 Cimbal, Walter/Stock Food/Olycom
Page 53 Dieterlen/Photolibrary.com
Page 55 Teubner Foodfoto/Stock Food/Olycom
Page 57 Sudres/Photolibrary.com
Page 59 FoodPhotogr.Eising/Stock Food/Olycom
Page 60 FoodPhotogr.Eising/Stock Food/Olycom
Page 61 Pfisterer, Walter/Stock Food/Olycom
Page 63 Teubner Foodfoto/Stock Food/Olycom
Page 65 Sudres Jean-Daniel/Photolibrary.com
Page 66 FoodPhotogr.Eising/Stock Food/Olycom
Page 67 Kopp, Ulrich/Stock Food/Olycom
Page 69 Nico Tondini/Photolibrary.com
Page 71 PrimaPress/Archivio Deagostini
Page 73 FoodPhotogr.Eising/Stock Food/Olycom
Page 75 Iden, K./Stock Food/Olycom
Page 77 FoodPhotogr.Eising/Stock Food/Olycom
Page 78 Cimbal, Walter/Stock Food/Olycom
Page 79 Norman Hollands/Photolibrary.com
Page 85 Sudres/Sucrè Salè/Tips Images
Page 87 Radvaner/Sucrè Salè/Tips Images
Page 89 Rivière/Sucrè Salè/Tips Images
Page 91 Teubner Foodfoto/Stock Food/Olycom
Page 93 Maximilian Stock Ldt/Stock Food/Olycom
Page 95 Vasseur, Frederic/Stock Food/Olycom
Page 97 Ryman/Sucrè Salè/Tips Images
Page 99 Sirois/Sucrè Salè/Tips Images
Page 101 Lawton/Sucrè Salè/Tips Images
Page 103 Jaqui Blanchard Photography/Stock Food/Olycom

Page 105 Brauner, Michael/Stock Food/Olycom
Page 107 Marielle/Photolibrary.com
Page 109 Princet, Aline/Stock Food/Olycom
Page 111 Tim Hill/Fabfoodpix.com
Page 113 Carol Sharp/Photolibrary.com
Page 115 Newedel, Karl/Stock Food/Olycom
Page 117 Tim Hill/Fabfoodpix.com
Page 119 Joff Lee/Photolibrary.com
Page 121 Peter Brooks/Photolibrary.com
Page 123 Nico Tondini/Photolibrary.com
Page 129 Foodcollection/Stock Food/Olycom
Page 131 Tim Hill/Fabfoodpix.com
Page 133 Miller, Elli/Stock Food/Olycom
Page 135 Anthony Blake/Photolibrary.com
Page 137 Nico Tondini/Photolibrary.com
Page 139 Caste/Sucrè Salè/Tips Images
Page 141 Jacqui Blanchard Photography/Stock Food/Olycom
Page 143 Tim Hill/Fabfoodpix.com
Page 145 Tim Hill/Fabfoodpix.com
Page 147 Martin Brigdale/Photolibrary.com
Page 148 FoodPhotogr.Eising/Stock Food/Olycom
Page 149 Dinodia Photo Library Pvt.Ltd/Stock Food/Olycom
Page 150 Moretto, Alberto/Stock Food/Olycom
Page 151 Ida, Akiko/Stock Food/Olycom
Page 153 Tim Hill/Fabfoodpix.com
Page 154 Gaurier/Sucrè Salè/Tips Images
Page 155 Dieterlen/Sucrè Salè/Tips Images
Page 156 left Moretto, Alberto/Stock Food/Olycom
Page 156 FoodPhotogr.Eising/Stock Food/Olycom
Page 157 FoodPhotogr.Eising/Stock Food/Olycom
Page 159 Foodfolio Studios/Digistock
Page 161 Tim Hill/Fabfoodpix.com
Page 163 Hilden Smith, Eva/Stock Food/Olycom
Page 164 MIXA Co.Ltd./Photolibrary.com
Page 167 Minowa Studio Co./Stock Food/Olycom
Page 169 Rivière/Sucrè Salè/Tips Images
Page 171 Bichon/Sucrè Salè/Tips Images
Page 173 Minowa Studio Co./Stock Food/Olycom
Page 175 Wieder, Frank/Stock Food/Olycom
Page 177 Jason Lowe/Photolibrary.com
Page 179 Garlick,Ian/Stock Food/Olycom
Page 181 FoodPhotogr.Eising/Stock Food/Olycom
Page 183 Tim Hill/Fabfoodpix.com
Page 185 Nico Tondini/Photolibrary.com
Page 187 Thelma&Louise/Stock Food/Olycom
Page 189 Food&Drink/Sucrè Salè/Tips Images
Page 193 Lister,Louise/Stock Food/Olycom
Page 195 Tim Hill/Fabfoodpix.com
Page 197 Geoff Higgins/Photolibrary.com
Page 199 Fleurent/Photolibrary.com
Page 201 Cazals,Jean/Stock Food/Olycom
Page 203 Batchelor,Ian/Stock Food/Olycom
Page 205 FoodPhotogr.Eising/Stock Food/Olycom
Page 207 Inc Supestock/Photolibrary.com

Page 209 Powers,Michael/Stock Food/Olycom
Page 214 Z.Sandmann/Cimbal/Stock Food/Olycom
Page 215 Alak,Chris/Stock Food/Olycom
Page 217 Keller&Keller Photography/Stock Food/Olycom
Page 219 Bill Tchakirides/Photolibrary.com
Page 221 Wegner, Brigitte/Stock Food/Olycom
Page 223 Monkey Business Images Ldt/Photolibrary.com
Page 224 DeSanto,Thom/Stock Food/Olycom
Page 227 Caggiano Photography/Stock Food/Olycom
Page 229 Ed Carey/Cole Group/Photolibrary.com
Page 231 Food&Drink/Sucrè Salè/Tips Images
Page 233 Foodcollection/Stock Food/Olycom
Page 235 Food Image Source/Frank Rogozienski/Stock Food/Olycom
Page 237 Alkèmia/Stock Food/Olycom
Page 239 Nico Tondini/Photolibrary.com
Page 241 Schieren, Bodo A./Stock Food/Olycom
Page 245 Lawton/Sucrè Salè/Tips Images
Page 243 FoodPhotogr.Eising/Stock Food/Olycom
Page 247 Nico Tondini/Photolibrary.com
Page 249 Andrave,Gustavo/Stock Food/Olycom
Page 251 Andrave,Gustavo/Stock Food/Olycom
Page 253 JTB Photo/Photolibrary.com
Page 255 Nico Tondini/Photolibrary.com
Page 257 Tim Hill/Fabfoodpix.com
Page 259 Torri,Matteo/Stock Food/Olycom
Page 261 Tim Hill/Fabfoodpix.com
Page 263 Pendle,Carl/Stock Food/Olycom
Page 265 Eising,Susie M./Stock Food/Olycom
Page 267 Madamour,Christophe/Stock Food/Olycom

WHITE STAR PUBLISHERS

WS White Star Publishers® is a registered trademark property of Edizioni White Star s.r.l.

© 2011 Edizioni White Star s.r.l.
Via M. Germano, 10 - 13100 Vercelli, Italy
www.whitestar.it

Translation: Mary Doyle
Editing: Elizabeth Heath

ISBN 978-88-544-0608-7
1 2 3 4 5 6   15 14 13 12 11

Printed in China